To Whitney Said

Library of Congress Cataloging-in-Publication Data

Lamm, Michael, 1936-
Thunderbird 2002

132 pages, size 12.125 x 9.125 inches.
Includes index.
ISBN 0-932128-08-4

1. Ford automobile--Design and construction--History.
2. Ford Thunderbird. I. Lamm-Morada Inc. II. Title.

629.2222LAM   00-092654 CIP

Copyright © 2000

Lamm-Morada Inc.
Post Office Box 7607
Stockton, California 95267 U.S.A.
Phone (209) 931-1056
Fax (209) 931-5777
Website: http://www.LammMorada.com

CONTENTS

WHAT A CONCEPT!

Ford decided in 1997 to discontinue production of the then-current Thunderbird five-passenger coupe. Contributing factors included a changing economy and customer demand for something different.

But even before 1997 production ended,

a spontaneous, informal "skunkworks" sprang up inside Ford's Design Center and started to work on a revival. The first three people involved were planner Rich Kisler, engineer Don Warneke and designer Ted Finney. This tiny group had no authorization and no funding, but the skunkworks trio felt strongly that the Thunderbird name couldn't be allowed to merely slip away. The iconic Bird had too much magic; too many memories.

"As the idea started to snowball," says Warneke, "we either got hold of more people or else let it be known that we were working on a new Thunderbird, and people started knocking on our doors." Soon a dozen or so colleagues from various disciplines had joined the skunkworks.

Design sketches began under then-vice president Jack Telnack, left. Early concepts included true sports cars like Brian White's two-seater on the previous page and also sporty boulevard cruisers like Mark Gorman's concept drawing below.

Upon Telnack's retirement, J Mays, right, became Ford's design vice president. Mays continued to refine the two-seater Thunderbird concept. This is an edgier early sketch by designer Jim Smith.

Ted Finney, who was design chief of large and luxury cars in Ford's rear-wheel-drive studio, comments that, "I think we met once a week, sometimes twice, with the rest of the skunkworks team. Those guys were involved in getting the cost figures, in trying to see where we could build the car, trying to find out...there was a lot of commonality work going on. We wanted to see if we could develop this platform using existing platform components, so we had a number of guys working on that.

"And I'll tell you, in all of my 33-year career, this Thunderbird was one of the most rewarding projects I've ever worked on, because of the intensity with which the whole team attacked it. The willingness of this

Telnack appointed Doug Gaffka, right, to lead the new Thunderbird design team. Gaffka's goal was to recapture the flavor of the classic 1955-57 Bird. These sketches, with alternate grilles, were done by John Trickey.

small group of people to really do a downtown job...well, there was real emotion between all of us. We became very proud of what we were doing and also defensive of outside attackers. There were those, too, you know."

Finney's colleague, Doyle Letson, recalls, "At the very early stages, we were doing just conceptual sketches of what we thought a Thunderbird should look like. We were going all over the place." In one version, the Thunderbird became a true sports car; in others it bore resemblances to Birds of the 1960s. Some sketches depicted futuristic two-seaters, others were two-plus-twos.

But members of the skunkworks soon agreed that the next Thunderbird needed to go back to its roots; that the original, classic Early Bird carried the strongest,

Don Warneke, left, was an original member of the skunkworks team. The basic elements and shape of the 2002 car were starting to come out in Brian White's computer-generated sketch above.

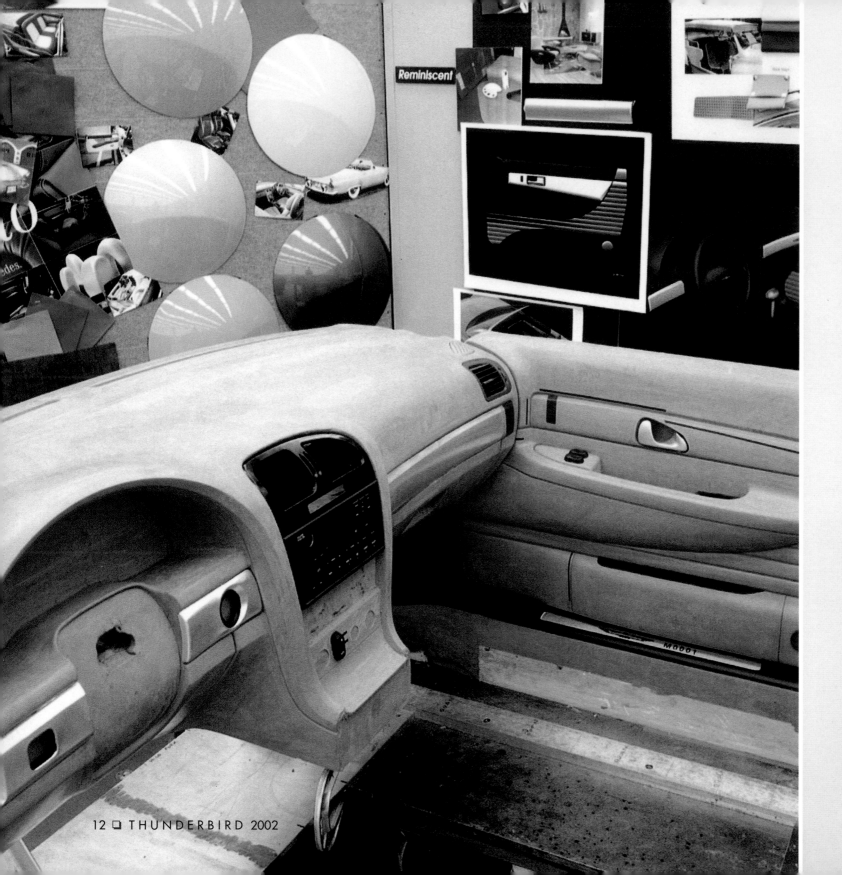

most evocative image the car ever enjoyed.

"As we started to narrow things down," Letson continues, "what really drove us—the direction—was that Dave Turner, Ford's rear-wheel-drive-car design director at the time, turned our attention to a couple of older Thunderbirds. Among other things, Dave used them to get Jac Nasser involved in the program; to get his support...." Nasser was head of product development at the time and later became president and CEO of Ford Motor Co.

❏ BUY TWO CLASSIC BIRDS
As the project developed, Thunderbird design chief Doug Gaffka authorized the purchase two vintage Birds, a 1955 and a

Mark Conforzi, right, headed T-Bird interior studio. Clay buck takes form, left, beneath a wall of 1955-57 color samples. Photo at right shows more finished stage of interior.

'57. After the cars arrived, both were parked inside the design studio, and Doug Gaffka suggested to his designers that they wash the cars to get a feel, literally, for the surfaces of these original Thunderbirds. "There's nothing like washing a car

to get familiar with it," maintains Gaffka.

Meanwhile, Jack Telnack points out that, "...one of the basic overall design cues of the original car was what we call the reverse wedge. The reverse wedge was

really essential to this new car. If you look at the silhouette of the 1955 T-Bird, it was high over the front fenders and dropped off toward the rear. That's very unlike today's cars, which mostly follow a wedge shape: low in front and higher in the rear. We felt that the reverse wedge was such an essential ingredient of the original car that we had to work with it."

Once they'd baked the general theme, the designers had something they could sink their teeth into. "One of the things that came out of our early discussions," explains Letson, "was the fact that we wanted this new car to be instantly recognizable from 100 yards away. We wanted to be able to have it turn the corner a block down the street and you'd know immediately what it was.

"So we started looking at what cues we wanted to pick up from the original to make that happen," Letson continues. "One was definitely the attitude of the vehicle, the lower rear and higher front. It was interesting...one evening we'd covered the original '55 and '57 with silk, just to cover them up in the studio at the end of the day, and looking at those shapes under the tarps told us what we wanted for the new car, because it was so easy to identify the old cars as Thunderbirds."

Clean bodysides, round tail lamps and squarish wheel cutouts characterized early clay model from Ford's Ghia studio.

At this point, though, the two-seater remained just so much pie in the sky. It still had no official sanction, and the people doing it remained on their own. But Rich Kisler and his financial planning people were starting to take a look at some of the money aspects. Kisler began with a proposal for another vehicle—a new, unapproved sport-coupe program, trying, as he puts it, "to be smart about using hardware that was then under development." He had in mind the company's desire to use key components tuned specifically to that vehicle.

"When we took our study to Jac Nasser," Kisler continues, "Jac

All these full-sized clay models have wraparound windshields. This one's facial expression tries to emulate original T-Bird's thrusting front end.

popped the question: Could you do a Thunderbird using the new architecture that was then under development? Of course, we didn't have hardware to work from, but we knew what the architecture was going to be. So my response to Jac's question, which got a lot of laughter, was, 'Piece of cake.' Jac talked to Ken Kohrs [Kohrs, an engineer, was vice president of Ford's large and luxury vehicle center] after the meeting, and Ken told me to come back and see him in a month.

"We brought back three proposals using relatively common hardware for the Thunderbird off that evolving platform. The one we recommended working on was a roadster. The other proposals, we felt, might be too much like the car that was still on the street, and people might not understand that we'd done a much better job with the hardware, so the next car could fall back into the same abyss that the present car was in.

"We decided that if we were going to do this, it had to be something really different. And Jac being Jac challenged us on several fronts, not the least of which was the investment. We then had to come back and see him in another couple of months, and one of the things we did was to benchmark the Puma in Germany. We used that car as a benchmark in terms of cost and production processes, because the Puma involved about the same volume as the Thunderbird would be."

By this time, there were many more people in the company who wanted to see a two-seat Thunderbird happen. But there were also plenty of others against it. The program was anything but a shoo-in, as Kisler explains:

"We had friends everywhere: in marketing and sales, in advanced manufacturing particularly, who helped us develop a proposal in a couple of months. Again, this was all very hypothetical and theoretical, because we didn't have hardware to go with it. But we developed enough of a proposal to say we could see light at the end of the tunnel. We now knew we could do a relatively low-volume car efficiently, and we took that news back to Jac Nasser and Ken Kohrs."

At that point, the skunkworks had invested a lot of enthusiasm in the project, but it still wasn't in what Ford calls "the cycle plan." A cycle plan lays out the developmental process of a new-car program. "Long story short," Kisler continues, "between then and the time Nancy Gioia picked up the program, we went through our typical gyrations of how much money do we have to spend in our cycle plan for forward model product, and the program went in and out of

the cycle plan maybe four or five times. It was always on the hit list.

"Ultimately, in my opinion, there's no way that the new Thunderbird would have happened without Jac Nasser. He was very, very instrumental, and if anyone were to ask who's responsible for this car, I'd lay it right at his doorstep. He had the political influence to make it happen, because there were a lot of people who did not want to do this car. I fought

hard battles...have letters in my files from people who didn't want the car, and they were very vocal about not going ahead with it.

"Nevertheless, in January before Nancy picked up the program, I had shut down the Ford model team I had running on it, because it looked like it was on the outs and wasn't going to come back in again. Then in January, I'm guessing that Jac took it to the board of directors and recommend-

ed that we do this project. I think he got a lot of enthusiastic response.... This was something new and exciting, and I think there was a lot of enthusiasm at that point. That's when the switch turned back on again, bigtime."

But a lot of questions remained. Was the new car going to indeed use architecture still under development? Or mightn't it be more practical from a manufacturing standpoint and more economical to do it on a different platform?

"Once the program was acknowledged," remarks Don Warneke, "the front-wheel-drive design studio did a version of the Thunderbird, and we did one in the rear-drive studio. It went through the normal beauty contests, but ours remained strong."

At that stage, any number of different studios submitted con-cept sketches. In addition to those from the two Dearborn groups, Ford's California studio plus Ford designers in Germany and Italy also made proposals, both rear- and front-wheel drive. According to Jack Telnack, "The Ghia design was very Italianate, the German version had a Teutonic look, but the only thing I wanted Teutonic about the car was the tread and the stance. The rest of it had to be pure American, but American for the 21st century, and with a technical bent."

Ford conducted a number of research clinics on both coasts, where a typical American audience was asked to choose among several different full-sized clay models of the Thunderbird, including those from California, Italy and Germany. The consensus confirmed Telnack's and Turner's own personal choice, that of the heritage two-seater.

On those rare occasions when Telnack or Turner invited guests into the studio—for example, Telnack's friend, yacht designer Tom Fexas—everyone, without fail, immediately recog-nized the car as a Thunderbird. So that goal—to make it instantly and decisively recognizable at a

More rounded wheel cutouts and character lines along the bodysides began to capture the classic Thunderbird look.

as: 1) a true sports car; 2) as a pure-ly retro design intended to simulate the 1955-57 Bird as literally as pos-sible; and finally, 3) he looked at what had already been done, namely the highly recognizable modern ren-dition of the classic two-seater. Within days, Gaffka decided to stick with the third alternative. He rea-soned that, "...if someone really wants an old classic Thunderbird, let him go buy the real thing, because a good one will cost about the same [as the new car]."

Gaffka points out that he and

Designers lightened up this more rounded version's heavy appearance with argent cladding along the rockers and bumpers.

distance—certainly had been met.

Ted Finney retired in 1997, as did Dave Turner. Turner's place as studio chief was taken by Doug Gaffka, whose previous job was to oversee the design of the 1992 and 1996 Tauruses. Late in 1997, Telnack asked Gaffka to step for-ward and take over what was essentially work in progress. The decision had been made to devel-op the Thunderbird from a platform then in use, but the final form left plenty of questions.

Gaffka started by examin-ing three avenues of design. He looked at the future Thunderbird

his T-Bird designers had to be cautious about one thing. "When you start copying some piece of the original, it can become a cartoon rather than a modern interpretation." The tail lamps serve as one example. "Jac Nasser wanted round lamps at any cost," explains Gaffka. "He really pushed for that, and he's right, too. It's very 'Thunderbird image.' I searched for other ways to do round tail lamps...is there a new way of putting a twist on a round lamp...what else can we do? Finally, we went to the round lamps that leaned back. I think they look pretty good. A lot of people wanted them to stand up, but when we tried them that way, they just looked old. We also looked at horizontal lamps for a while, but we got off that pretty quickly. They just weren't in char-

Wall-mounted studies for silver-on-black Neiman Marcus Edition helped Thunderbird designers tailor interior and exterior detailing.

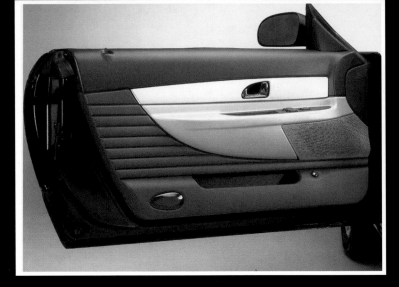

The idea was to distinguish the Neiman Marcus Edition with restrained luxury.

Final version of Neiman Marcus cars ended up with silver shift knobs and steering wheel plus Thunderbird emblems on instrument panel and floor mats.

acter—took us too much into the '60s and '70s."

Soon after Gaffka's appointment, Jack Telnack retired, and his place as Ford's design vice president was taken by J Mays. Mays had been a consultant to the company and, as such, he'd already influenced the Thunderbird's design indirectly. Ted Finney remembers a presentation that Mays gave at Detroit's Rattlesnake Club in which

he helped define the character and brand imaging of the Thunderbird. Mays himself says that he'd seen the various Italian, German, California and Dearborn designs and felt they were all too intuitive and that there wasn't enough focus.

AT THE RATTLESNAKE CLUB

Mays has a way of translating verbal cues into visual ones. At the Rattlesnake Club presentation, he led the Thunderbird designers through the vehicle's defining characteristics. Mays has a knack for arranging words on a continuum and then carefully choosing those that apply to a particular car. For example, one of the things Mays talked about was the optimism of postwar America and how optimism was reflected in the original 1955-57 Thunderbird. So the continuum started with the word "optimism" at one end—cheerful, happy, confident in a rosy future—and at the other end of the spectrum was "somber" as a substitute for "pessimism."

Now in terms of visual cues, somber might be seen as sterile, dark, austere, lacking in texture,

When the $41,995 Neiman Marcus Edition went on sale by phone on September 25, 2000, all 200 cars were snapped up in two hours and 15 minutes.

angular, rigid, functional and straightforward. In vehicular terms, a hearse expresses the word "somber."

At the optimistic end of the spectrum, Mays mentioned that the visual cues would include bright, upbeat, inviting, non-conventional colors and silvery chrome. Fun, he says, plays an important role here.

Optimistic shapes are smoother and softer. The optimistic car has a more acceptable, more populist look than the somber hearse. That's one example of the sort of reasoning and the verbal/visual translations Mays was able to make.

Another word that kept popping up in Mays' discussion with T-Bird designers was "American."

That could mean a lot of things, but to narrow the definition in this case, the group adopted "bold, confident and free." And with that set of verbal cues, they decided the opposite would be "reserved."

In terms of sportiness, the design group settled on "relaxed sportiness" as opposed to "extreme sportiness." An example of relaxed

sportiness comes by looking at riders of different types of bicycles. A person riding a Schwinn of the 1950s sits upright and relaxed. His body stance is basically vertical. Contrast this with the racing-bike rider: rump in the air, face between low handle grips, a horizontal stance. The Schwinn bike implies relaxed sportiness; the racing bike

lamps [so they became] a graphic representation of the Dagmars on the original vehicle, but not quite so politically incorrect. And then we went from a black grille...to an aluminum eggcrate. I think that really helped bring the car to life."

At Mays' urging, the designers gave the front end more vee in plan view. In other words, if you look down on the car from directly above, the headlights and the outside edges of the front fenders got moved back, but the centerpoint stayed where it was. Mays felt this helped to visually soften the car's front overhang—made it less pronounced. "And we just spent days tuning lines and trying to get the tension and the acceleration of the lines to run the way we thought they should," he says.

The windshield presented a challenge not just to the designers but also to the engineers. "The problem," says Doyle Letson, "was manufacturability. You can get a wraparound windshield like the original, provided it's not compound-curved. If you look at the original 1955-57 windshield, it's just straight glass with wrapped corners. But in the new car, there'd be too much glass and too many compound curves. You'd end up with a lot of distortion."

Gaffka adds, "The windshield was a real piece of work. Originally we tried a wrapping effect, with pillars and vent windows, but that involved a lot of separate pieces and moldings. Even as it is now, the windshield took a tremendous amount of development. It's a really complicated shape."

❏ INTERIOR DESIGN NUANCES
The new Thunderbird's interior was done under the direction of Mark Conforzi, who'd spent eight years at Ford of Europe, where he'd worked on the Scorpio, Sierra and Escort. Conforzi had been invited to join the Dearborn design team specifically to create the interior.

makes the point: extreme sportiness.

When Mays entered the vice presidency, he felt that the Thunderbird was still burdened with a lot of mixed messages. The car, though, was too near completion to start over, so, "I saw my job as much as editor as design director," he states. "What we were looking for, front to back, was consistency of message." In that regard, he edited the headlights and tail lamps to make them look perfectly round. He edited the hood scoop so it didn't stick up like an upside-down metal box. He edited the character line down the bodyside so it didn't yell THUNDERBIRD but simply said *Thunderbird* with recognizable authority.

"We went from squarish, complicated wheel-well cutouts to very geometrical round ones," Mays continues. "We gave the car slightly more shoulder and slightly more wheel flare, and I'm talking here six to eight millimeters; not much. At the time, we also had quite a complicated front end, with a chrome bumper and some other stuff going on down below. We took all that off, and we integrated the fog

"We started with a clean sheet," says Conforzi, "and really didn't know at first what the interior should be like. There were only a few designers working with me at the time—Jim Smith was one, Rafael Rego was another. We wanted to come up with some type of dramatically new interior.

❏ A DASHING DASHBOARD
"At the time, we had a 1955 Thunderbird in the studio. I was familiar with past Thunderbirds, and I liked that. I wanted us to bring the heritage in as much as we could without making it look like a total retrocar. I felt the interior definitely had to be modern, because the exterior is modern. But we wanted elements from the past in there.

"One of the great things about the original car...you sit inside it, and there's so much metal and chrome everywhere. We wanted to get that feeling into this car. So we drew a lot of our inspiration from the original—1955-56-57 and even the early '60s. The exterior was coming pretty close to what it looks like today when we started to develop the interior. The exterior definitely influenced the interior; it set the tone."

The basic dash panel, including the instrument cluster and controls, is shared with the Lincoln LS, but the use of colors and textures sets the Thunderbird apart. "If you look at [the interiors of]...automobiles from the '50s," observes J Mays, "part of what made them exciting had nothing to do with the shape. It had to do with the multitude of colors, materials and textures. Those interiors were really a pastiche—almost a birthday cake—of materials and textures. So I wanted to bring a little of that back into the Thunderbird without doing it in such a retro way that we'd just end up with an old car.

"So we took this [Lincoln LS] instrument panel and broke it up into a triple-tone scheme, putting the color of the exterior into the

Sideview illustrates the rear-tapering, reverse-wedge silhouette. Concept-car interior, opposite, differed from production in color application and aluminum center stack.

We wanted to keep the Thunderbird interior contemporary and romantic in an upbeat way."

Regarding the instrument cluster, Conforzi's designers experimented with dial faces in black, metallic and white, including a warm, slightly yellowish shade of white. The background color they finally settled on is pure white with turquoise needles and silver dials.

Conforzi points out that he and his team also went through a lot of different designs for the seats. The original engineering concept was a self-contained seat with belts and side airbags integrated into the design. Conforzi's people began with fairly bulky-looking buckets but rejected them as too massive for the car. After several trials, they ended up with production seats that look very much like those in the 1999 Thunderbird showcars.

The finish on the Bird's center stack likewise took a bit of doing. (The center stack is that forward, upright continuation of the central console.) Initially, Conforzi wanted the center stack to be clad in brushed aluminum, and the

showcars came out that way. But feasibility studies showed that actual aluminum metal heavy enough to resist denting was too thick for pushbutton clearance. So Conforzi tried thin metal appliques. Those didn't work either.

"Finally we looked at different paints for the center stack," he notes. "Every week there were dozens of paints that we'd examine to see how closely we could match the aluminum. We came pretty close, but no matter what we did, it still looked like paint." They tried plastics. No good. Finally, they decided to go with a special black polymer surface for the center stack, and now it looks like what it is: plastic, but of very high quality.

The Thunderbird concept car made its first public appearance on 3 January 1999 at the North American International Auto Show at Cobo Hall in Detroit. Reaction was swift and overwhelmingly positive. The public and the motoring press were delighted by what they saw, which only reinforced Ford's resolve to go ahead with production of the 2002 Thunderbird.   ❏

lower panel, leaving the upper black, then taking off the wood of the LS and applying an aluminum panel there to mimic the classic Thunderbird's interior trim. And Mark Conforzi did a wonderful job in tying [the] instrument panel together with quite flamboyant door panels."

Corforzi adds that, "We

had an opportunity to do quite a number of different [door-panel] designs, because we didn't know whether we should really stretch toward the radical or go retro or do something in between. We did some machine-like door panels, similar to what was in the MY Mercury concept car. We struggled with that, but it was a bit too severe for this car.

Concept Thunderbird with removable top poses
on 17-Mile Drive, near Carmel, California.

chapter 2

ENGINEERING THE NEW BIRD

When time came to persuade Ford's decision-makers to revive the Thunderbird as a two-seater, Bob Widmer picked Nancy Gioia for the job. Widmer, who was the vehicle line director for large and luxury cars, recalls,

Helmeted test drivers put an early engineering prototype of the 2002 Thunderbird through its paces at Ford's Dearborn, Michigan test track.

"I learned early-on that it was good policy to put Nancy on the stage to make a pitch, because she's so convincing...so full of energy that I could never say no to her. She's a great spokesperson and a great ambassador for the Thunderbird legacy."

Nancy Gioia (pronounced JOY-ah) grew up in Livonia, Michigan, where her parents are both school teachers. Gioia is smart, charming, charismatic, driven by pride and upbringing in what used to be a man's world.

In high school, Gioia thought about becoming a lawyer. But a summer job with Ford, charting mass airflow data for fuel-injection systems, propelled her toward engineering. She enrolled at the University of Michigan and graduated in 1982 with a degree in electrical engineering. Fifteen companies wooed her; she chose Ford Motor Co.

Her timing was good. Onboard automotive electronics were just taking off. Gioia moved rapidly from circuit design to manufacturing, and Ford sent her to

Thunderbird floorpan received extra strengthening in tunnel and rocker areas.

Stanford to get a master's degree in manufacturing systems engineering. Ford then put her to work on a variety of projects, from manufacturing to supplier alliances to business and strategic planning. Nancy Gioia was chief program engineer for heavy-duty trucks when, in June 1997, Widmer asked her to take

the lead on the Thunderbird.

Gioia arrived two weeks before the Thunderbird's "Strategic Intent" presentation. Strategic intent is a milestone meeting where the advocates of a new program lay out the business case, engineering strategy and manufacturing ramifications.

The program hinged on being able to develop an architecture that would be unique to the Thunderbird. And everyone agreed that the new Thunderbird had to be engineered using state-of-the-art C3P tools. (C3P stands for CAD/CAM/CAE/PIM, meaning computer-aided design, computer-aided manufacturing, computer-aided engineering and product information management.)

"They [Widmer's group] had looked at other platforms," Gioia says. "There was a design contest between a total of three platform possibilities. Two were rear-wheel drive and one was front-drive. The question got down to: Should the next Thunderbird be front- or rear-wheel drive, and I

Nancy Gioia, right, served as the new Thunderbird's chief engineer. She and her former boss, Ken Kohrs, left, were instrumental in choosing to use a rear-wheel-drive platform for the 2002 Thunderbird.

think the fundamentalists said, 'You cannot do a front-drive Thunderbird. It must be rear-drive, and it has to have a V8. Beyond the business case, I think the essence of the brand came through, and we

said it had to be rear drive," she recalls.

"By looking at each rear-wheel-drive platform, its age, its technical capabilities going forward," Gioia continues, "we real-

ized how much more had already been done in the area of chassis dynamics work and structure in the latest architecture being developed for the Lincoln LS. So we decided to make that the platform we'd move

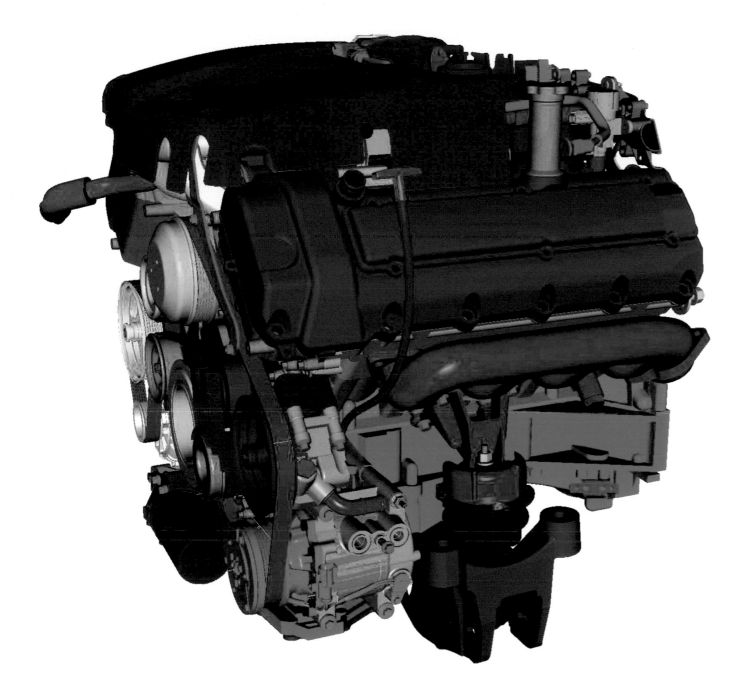

T-Bird's 3.9-liter aluminum V8 has twin overhead camshafts on each bank and four valves per cylinder, delivers a smooth 252 horsepower.

from." And that's how Gioia presented the case at the strategic intent meeting.

She made such a convincing presentation that the powers that be, including Jac Nasser, who'd recently become president and CEO of Ford Motor Co., endorsed the rear-drive architecture for the convertible and, by the end of June 1997, the new Thunderbird was off and running. Ken Kohrs, vice president of Ford's large and luxury vehicle center at the time, then appointed Nancy Gioia as Thunderbird chief program engineer, so it became her job to get the car on the road.

"Gioia came up with a very innovative single prototype program," comments Kohrs. "Usually you have two waves of prototypes made from prototype tools. It's an expensive process. Prototype vehicles usually cost between $500,000 and $1 million each.

"But Gioia said we weren't going to do that this time. We were going to design the vehicle largely on the computer, because we had a great breadth of computer data that

Returnless fuel-injection system, left, reduces tank vapors, thus emissions. Red exhaust catalysts, below, stand near engine, so they heat quickly to cut cold-start emissions.

we gathered during the development of other vehicles; we knew a lot about the platform, and we would do production tools from the beginning and go right to production-tooled prototypes."

The new platform presented some early challenges, as Kohrs points out. "The original 1955-57 Thunderbird, when you look at it in silhouette, has a very long hood and a short rear deck. The evolving platform was almost the opposite: cab forward, short hood, wheels at the corners, so we had a difficult time creating the look of the modern interpretation of the old Thunderbird."

So the Thunderbird team did an innovative job of moving the door hinge pillars toward the rear. They designed a wall for the T-Bird hinge pillars to move the door cutline back. If they

Hydraulic cooling fan, left, is driven by a pump, below, that provides 80% more power than an electric fan. Variable fan speed makes for more efficient cooling and less noise.

A/C components are tightly packaged ahead of radiator. Hydraulic pump also drives fan for air-conditioning condenser.

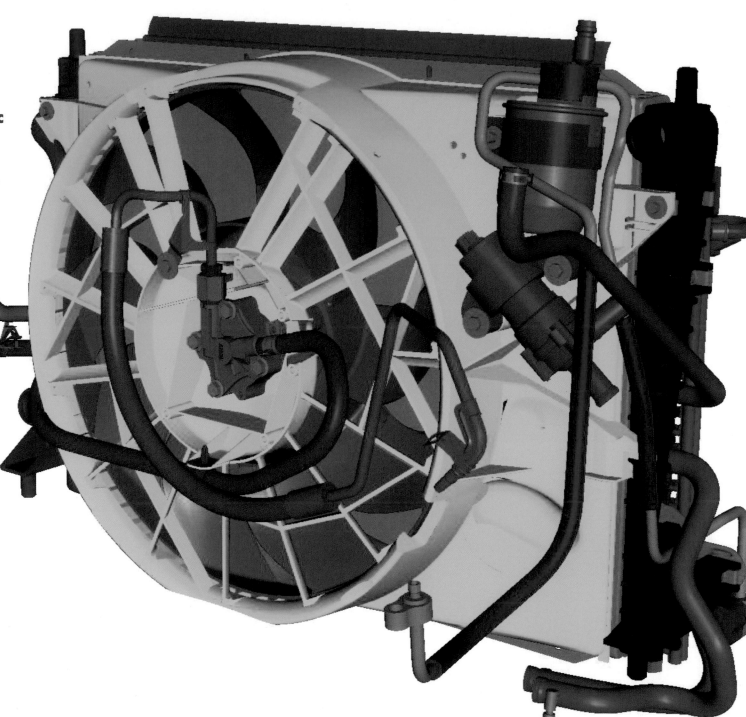

hadn't done this, the Thunderbird's doors would have ended up being uncomfortably long and unwieldy.

Body engineers, under Peter Kantz, also did a lot of work with windshield shape and rake to make the new Thunderbird look like the old car when, in fact, the glass had to be totally different. Unlike most modern windshields, the hot glass is pressed in a mold rather than draped over a form and shaped by gravity. The pressure-molding process allows more of the classic wraparound look, and the windshield rake, at 64 degrees, is much "faster" (leaned-back) than in most modern cars.

The Thunderbird platform was arrived at by using Ford Motor Co.'s latest vehicle architecture. The result was a 107.2-inch wheelbase for the T-Bird versus 114.5 inches on other Ford products that use similar architecture. The team's engineers were able to shorten the center section of the floorpan by 7.3 inches while still delivering a solid base to work from. And Gioia says that her greatest challenge involved building the proper amount of rigidity into the Thunderbird chassis. Her goal was to make the overall structure as stiff and strong as possible.

Viscous engine mount, shown in blue, contains oil and keeps noise and vibrations from reaching passenger compartment.

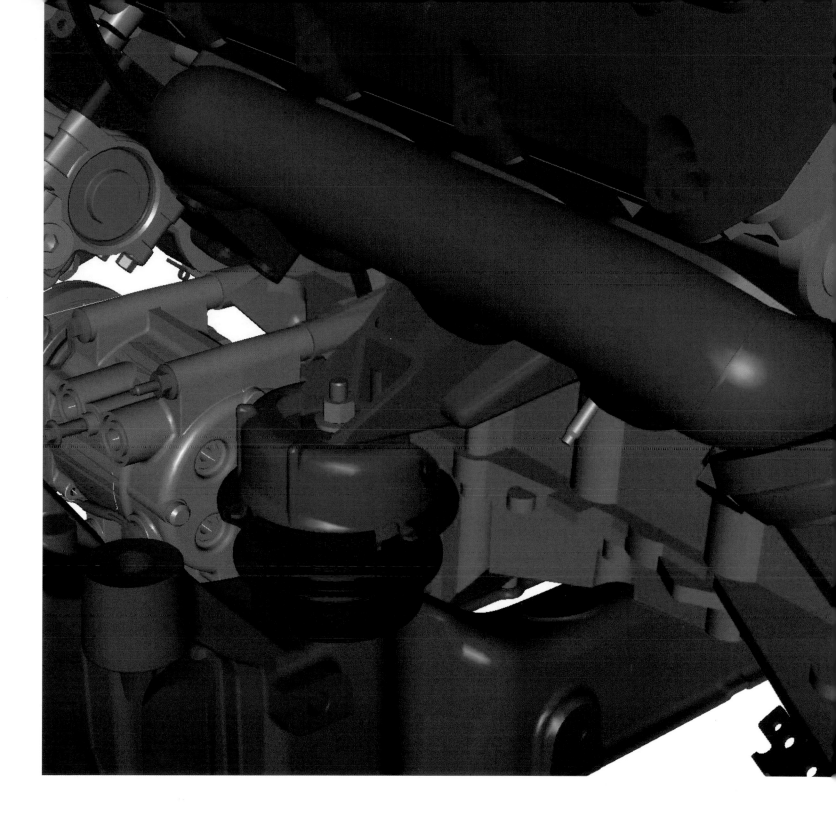

"When you have a closed car," she notes, "and you take the top off, your body integrity changes a lot. So we had to enhance structural rigidity. We up-gauged the rocker sections, strengthened the A-pillar hinge attachment points and developed a unique windshield header."

The three-piece platform

All Thunderbirds come with a five-speed automatic transmission.

allowed Gioia's team to put thicker-gauge steel into sections that would see higher torsional loads. For added strength, Thunderbird engineers added crossmembers under the chassis to improve handling.

The chassis rocker rails–

Dual front crossmembers, the blue one steel and the brown one aluminum, support radiator, engine and aluminum suspension arms.

those raised areas under the doors—contain tubular steel inner reinforcements. Behind the rocker rails are fully boxed steel sections that run back alongside the trunk. There's another cross-car reinforcement behind the seats plus hefty steel beams inside the doors to protect against side impacts.

Front section of two-piece driveshaft is a hollow tube that collapses rather than breaking on impact. Center support bearing, below, is rubber mounted to minimize driveline vibrations.

A steel rear subframe attaches to the floorpan and carries the rear suspension, differential housing, axles and disc brakes. Big rubber donuts isolate the subframe from the body and suspension system. This helps minimize road noise and harshness.

The Thunderbird uses under-

Steel rear subrame carries aluminum suspension arms, arrives at plant pre-assembled with axle halfshafts and brakes (not shown). Below, extensive use of multiplexing characterizes Thunderbird's electrical system.

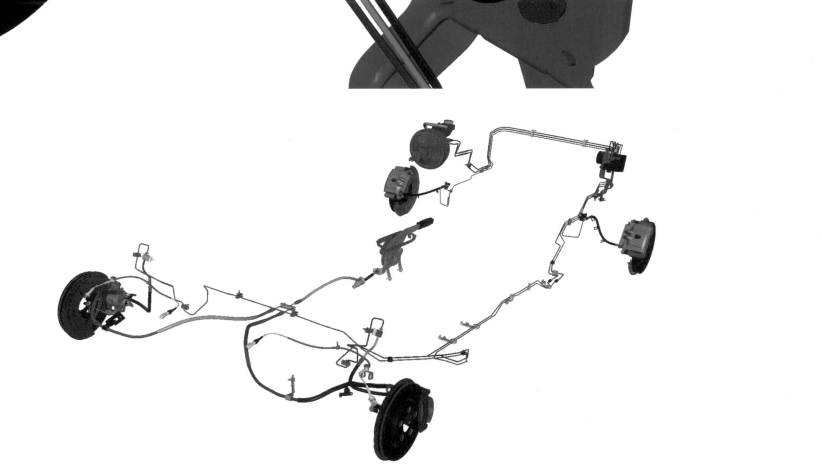

All T-Bird brake rotors are vented and make use of a four-channel antilock system. ABS pump is shown above right. ABS also provides brake proportioning, eliminating the need for a proportioning valve. Suspension is set up with anti-dive geometry.

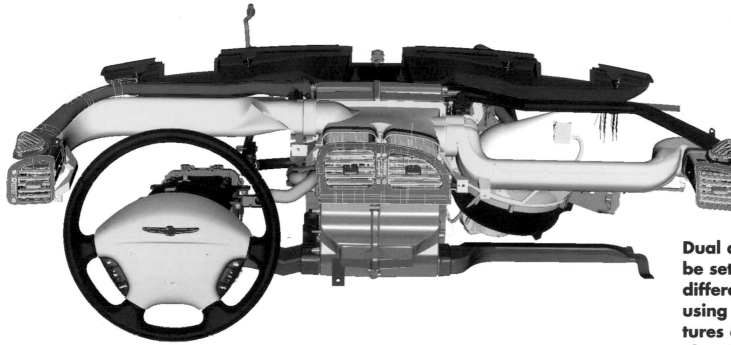

Dual automatic climate control can be set by driver and passenger for different temperatures. Intead of using air-blend doors, temperatures are regulated by a single, electrically controlled valve.

body X-braces front and rear, a cross-car beam behind the seats, reinforcements in the door hinge pillars, door frames, lock strikers and rear floor sidemembers. The windshield pillars and header are double walled, with corner castings for the top clamps. The end result is an extremely robust, solid body/chassis structure.

Ford Motor Co.'s new vice president of North American Car,

Chris Theodore, became a zealot for fit, finish and build quality. In the final two years of the T-Bird's development, Theodore, fresh from DaimlerChrysler, challenged the team to question their assumptions and conclusions in pursuit of what he called "Bugatti" execution: stunning appearance in addition to flawless craftsmanship.

The Thunderbird's drivetrain consists of an all-aluminum, twin-

cam, 32-valve, 3.9-liter V8 engine and five-speed automatic transmission. The two-piece driveshaft uses rubber flex couplings at both ends, and the center support bearing has rubber dampers to help isolate vibrations.

The Thunderbird engine delivers 252 bhp at 6000 rpm and 267 ft. lb. of torque at 4250 rpm. As in other premium Ford vehicles, the T-Bird uses oil-filled, viscous

motor mounts to help isolate engine harshness and vibrations.

The new Bird's fuel-injection system is unusual in that it doesn't need a return line. Instead, the onboard powertrain computer monitors how much fuel the engine needs for any given task and adjusts the flow accordingly from the Thunderbird's kidney-shaped tank. The returnless system reduces weight, complexity and emissions.

Leather seats have six-way power adjustments on the driver's side and two-way power on the passenger's. Standard side airbags are mounted in both side bolsters and deploy between the seats and doors. Seatbacks recline and tilt forward.

The Thunderbird engine uses a classic dual exhaust system. Each bank of the V8 has a separate, twin-walled exhaust header plus its own catalytic converter, muffler and resonator. The exhaust note has been tuned to sound as much as possible like the classic Thunderbird.

"We went so far as to get audio tapes of the original Thunderbird," says Gioia, "in order to graph the tone and volume. It actually worked out well for us, because we reduced exhaust back pressure and got a little more horse-power that way."

The 32-bit powertrain computer has one megabyte of ROM and monitors not just the engine but also automatic transmission shifts, the cruise control, alternator (no voltage regulator needed) and hydraulic cooling fan. The fan is powered by a pump driven off the engine's accessory belt. The big advantage, when you compare this hydraulic fan with a conventional electric type, is 80% more shaft torque than a belt-driven pump. This allows the blades to push 30% more air through the radiator core and air-conditioner condenser. The onboard computer automatically adjusts fan speed for the quietest, most efficient operation.

The five-speed automatic transmission, coded 5R55N, is actually a six-speed. But the ratio that would have been fifth gear was deemed redundant, so this gearbox ended up with five working ratios, the top one an overdrive. There's a French connection here. The transmission is made in Ford's Sharonville, Ohio plant, but some internal parts come from the company's gear facility in Bordeaux, France.

The Thunderbird's suspension, as on some Ferraris and other exotic sports cars, uses independent short and long arms (SLA) at all four corners. This means that at each corner, two A-shaped suspension members attach to the chassis, one above the other, with coil springs in between. Inside the coils are double-walled shock absorbers.

Many suspension components are made from aircraft-quality cast aluminum, including the steering knuckles and forged front con-

trol arms. Front and rear stabilizer bars limit lean during hard cornering, and aluminum helps keep unsprung suspension weight down for better ride and handling. The car has nearly 50/50 weight distribution, so it's extremely well balanced.

Engineering supervisor Steve Akers and his group set up the new Thunderbird's suspension to limit rear lift under hard braking. Normally, when you stop a car quickly, weight shifts forward, the car's nose dives and the rear lifts. As a result, the front tires end up doing most of the braking. But engineers under Akers set up the Thunderbird's SLA suspension with 125% anti-lift geometry, so that the upper and lower control-arm pivot planes force the entire car down toward the roadway during hard braking. This equalizes the braking forces on all four tires. On hard acceleration, the car rises slightly.

Steering is by variable-ratio rack and pinion with variable power assist. At speed, the variable rack makes it easy for the driver to hold a straight line without constant

Standard soft top and optional removable top have heated glass rear windows. Removable top comes with wheeled aluminum storage cart.

Steel doors contain side-guard beams. Interior door panels house storage binnacles and speakers.

little inputs. Then for parking, the steering gear ratio speeds up as the steering wheel rotates, thereby taking fewer revolutions to turn the front tires. The variable power assist adds hydraulic muscle during slow, tight maneuvers like parking. The amount of assist decreases at speed so the driver gets a better feel of the road.

Brakes are discs all around: 11.8-inch vented rotors in front and 11.3-inchers aft. The aluminum front calipers have twin pistons. A four-channel antilock braking system is standard. ABS keeps a car's wheels from locking up during panic stops, allowing the driver to steer during hard braking. Steering isn't possible with the front tires locked up. And in the Thunderbird, ABS also functions as the brake proportioning valve. An optional all-speed traction control system works in conjunction with ABS to prevent wheelspin on slippery road surfaces.

The 2002 Thunderbird offers 17 x 7.5-inch cast-aluminum wheels in two finishes: painted (standard) and chrome plated (optional). These are "Euro flange" wheels, meaning the front face of the rim has a minimal wheel lip. Adhesive balance weights go on the wide, flat rear inner wheel flange so they're out of sight. Tires are V-rated P235/50VR17 all-season blackwalls, with an aluminum mini spare under the trunk floor. The fully lined, 9.1-cubic-foot trunk can hold two sets of golf clubs.

The Budd Co., which built the all-steel bodies for the 1955-57 T-Birds, supplies the hood, decklid and front fenders for this latest generation. These parts are made from sheet-molded compound (SMC), a type of tough, durable plastic. The rest of the body is steel and is made by Ford. Stampings for all sheetmetal components—rear fenders, the "black metal" underbody, wheelhouses, upper back panels—are engineered to need only one strike on Ford's single-stitch finishing press. On other cars, most metal stampings need two or three strikes and as many different presses to bend them into their final shape. Also, the Thunderbird uses fewer stamping dies than most vehicles.

The 2002 Thunderbird comes with a soft top as standard equipment, with an optional lift-off top. Engineering supervisor Denis Kansier used premium luxury sportsters like the Jaguar XK8 as his targeting benchmarks for the soft top. Kansier wanted an automatic top that worked and looked better than any of the benchmark cars. The result is a one-button switch to raise and lower the top and a one-handle latch to lock and release it from the windshield header.

The Thunderbird top uses three layers of material over a four-bow frame. The outer layer is a tough, acrylic Landmark woven fabric stitched with acrylic thread. The fabric has an elastomer undersurface and a polymer/cotton backing. Then there's the soft top's middle layer, which consists of an acoustical and thermal insulating foam material. This helps keep the outer layer smooth. The innermost layer—the headliner—is gray finishing cloth. The top itself folds nearly flat and is covered by a three-layer vinyl boot that snaps in place.

The soft-top mechanism is powered by an electric pump and two hydraulic cylinders. The light-weight front or "header" bow is made of cast aluminum. To attach the header bow to the windshield, a central handle clamps two J-hooks to the tops of the A-pillars. It takes only six pounds of force to activate or release this clamp handle, and it's specifically designed not to pinch or scrape fingernails.

The glass rear window is larger than in most convertible tops, and it's electrically heated to melt snow and ice. The electrical contacts are embedded in the top itself, and a sensor can tell the car's central computer whether the top is up or down so that the glass isn't accidentally heated with the top stowed.

Engineer Sean Strine had responsibility for the optional, removable top. The top is made of two layers of SMC and weighs 80 pounds. Depending on the customer's wishes, removable tops are painted either white or the same color as the car and have a foam-backed black headliner.

The lift-off top comes with three standard accessories: an alu-

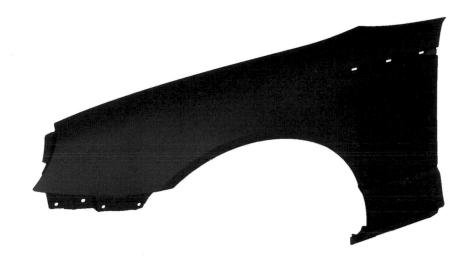

Front fenders are made of sheet-molded compound (SMC) to reduce weight, resist rust and denting.

minum storage cart for wheeling the top around a garage, a Torx-head bolt tool to attach the top to the windshield header, and a fitted fabric cover. The cover is perforated, so it "breathes" and can't trap water.

The removable top has U-channel weatherseals, same as the soft top. In addition to the two Torx-head bolts that fasten the top to the windshield header, two clamp latches in back draw the top down onto soft seals around the bottom lip. Electronic module sensors recognize the removable top and deactivates the switch for raising and lowering the soft top.

There's also a switch on the center stack to deactivate the right-side airbag; for example, when a child sits in the passenger's seat.

The steering column tilts and telescopes electrically at the touch of a button. The wheel itself contains fingertip switches for the cruise control and sound system. The six-way power driver's seat and two-way power passenger's seat both have

manual lumbar adjustments and standard side airbags.

The central driveshaft tunnel contains shielding to keep heat and noise from the powertrain and exhaust from entering the cabin. Six separate shields run from the toe-board area back to the differential. Also, the top of the cowl is filled with polyurethane foam to help damp noise.

The Thunderbird has an automatic dual-mode climate control system. This means that the driver and passenger can program two different temperature settings into the display, and the system will deliver airflow at those temperatures to the right and left sides of the cockpit. Or if only the driver is in the car, he or she can switch to single mode and only one preset air temperature enters the entire car.

If the two temp settings are too far apart—say 68 degrees

Fahrenheit for the driver and 90 degrees for the passenger—the system automatically favors the driver. The system also chooses outside air or recirculated air automatically. And instead of opening and shutting little air-blend doors, temperatures are controlled by electric stepper motors that selectively open and close valves in the heater core and air-conditioner evaporator.

The climate-control display registers the outside temperature, and two separate sun-load sensors on the dashboard can read temperature differences between the driver's and passenger's side of the car. That helps the automatic system decide which valves to open and close to keep both occupants comfortable.

Finally, the 2002 Thunderbird comes with an amazing 200-watt Audiophile sound system. It has eight speakers, including an 80-watt subwoofer assembly, plus an in-dash, six-disc CD changer. An equalization selector allows the sound to be tailored for top-up or top-down operation, for the driver only or for both driver and pas-

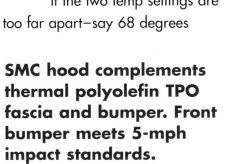

SMC hood complements thermal polyolefin TPO fascia and bumper. Front bumper meets 5-mph impact standards.

senger. Digital sound processing can simulate the effects of a concert hall, a sports stadium or jazz club. And volume automatically gets louder the faster the car goes, a feature taken from the original 1955-57 Thunderbird radio.

The receiver has presets for six AM and 12 FM stations. The antenna is embedded in the windshield glass, so there's no mast to snag when you put on or take off the removable top. A full complement of audio switches on the steering wheel means the driver never has to look away to turn the sound system on or off, change stations or operate the CD changer.

So Nancy Gioia and her engineering staff brought to life a highly advanced and different sort of American dreamcar. The 2002 Thunderbird appears destined to become a classic in the same way as the first T-Birds from nearly half a century ago. ❏

Ford vice president Chris Theodore checks T-Bird prototype for body fits.

A Sampler of Innovations

The 2002 Thunderbird contains a number of thoughtful engineering touches and conveniences. Among them:

❑ **Electrical multiplexing.** Instead of using one wire for each electrical function, this new technology lets a wire carry signals for several different functions. In the 2002 Thunderbird, multiplexing cuts the number of individual wires approximately in half—to 250 from 500. Advantages of multiplexing include simpler electrical circuitry, fewer connectors, fewer chances to mis-wire during assembly, lighter wires because they carry information rather than heavy current, thinner insulation, longer switch life and greater durability.

❑ **Autolamp.** Autolamp features a sensor that measures the amount of natural light outside the car and automatically turns on the headlights when it starts to get dark.

❑ **Battery saver.** Headlights or fog lamps that are left on will automatically turn off 10 minutes after the key is taken out of the ignition.

❑ **Smart door locks.** If the key is inadvertently left in the ignition, the doors won't lock.

❑ **Speed-sensitive windshield wipers.** The wipers speed up as the car goes faster.

❑ **Window drop.** If the side windows are shut, they automatically lower half an inch or so whenever you open the door or raise/lower the convertible top. This is to prevent the glass from catching in the inverted-U-shaped rubber window channels. With the doors shut and/or the top up, the glass automatically rises again to give a tight seal. The U-shaped channel holds the glass in place at speed, when air pressure tries to push the side windows outward and away from the seals.

❑ **Battery in trunk.** Stowing the battery in the trunk helps the Thunderbird get its near 50/50 weight distribution.

❑ **Heated rear window.** Both the cloth top and the removable top have electrically heated glass rear windows.

❑ **Fail-safe cooling.** In the unlikely event that the engine loses coolant, you could still drive a reasonable distance to the nearest service

garage. The engine computer, sensing the coolant loss, would alternate cylinder firing to prevent overheating.

❑ **Block heater.** An electrical engine block heater is standard equipment for 2002 Thunderbirds sold in Canada and optional elsewhere.

❑ **Glovebox hook.** A folding hook on the glovebox door makes a handy place to hang a purse or other items.

❑ **Dual trip odometers.** The Thunderbird has two trip odometers. One allows you to keep track of, say, oil-change intervals while the other might record the miles traveled on a business trip.

❑ **SecuriLock.** The Thunderbird's ignition system uses an electronic capsule embedded in the key. To start the car, the ignition lock has to recognize this capsule. If it doesn't, the engine won't start. To be sure no one can replicate the key, the system randomly changes the coding each time the engine starts. To make a repeat code unlikely, there are 72 million billion combinations! ❑

Thunderbird Suppliers

Independent suppliers played an important role in the development of the 2002 Thunderbird. Ford Motor Co., like other U.S. automakers, relies on suppliers to help engineer the parts they supply.

According to Mike O'Sullivan, who was Ford's purchasing director for advanced programs, "In the past, Ford traditionally had legions of engineers who did all the design and development of every component in every car we built. Once the design of a given part was completed, it was turned over to purchasing, and purchasing sent it out for bids from our various suppliers.

"Today, we've shifted to much more engineering reliance on the suppliers themselves. They have the expertise, after all, in building that component, especially since they supply more than one auto manufacturer. So we expect the supplier to bring to the table all the creativity that it takes to engineer a given part. We also expect him to be able to build that part to the standards of quality and reliability that we expect.

"So there's a joint investment here. We both want the vehi-

cle to succeed, because if it does, everyone wins. We sell more cars, and the supplier gets more business. The supplier thus has a stake in the car and its success; a commitment to quality and good engineering. We view the supplier as an extension of our enterprise.

"And nowadays, when I sit in a meeting, I often don't know who works for Ford and who works for the supplier. The supplier's engineers work so closely with our own engineers that they even occupy the same rooms and laboratories within product development."

As Thunderbird production began, the following companies supplied these components, usually as drop-in subassemblies:

❏ Lear Corp.: complete interior: seats, door panels, carpeting, hard trim and removable top headliner.

❏ Visteon Automotive Systems: instrument panel.

❏ Prince Corp.: tunnel console.

❏ Budd Co.: SMC hood, decklid, front fenders.

❏ Venture Industries Corp.: removable top.

❏ North American Lighting: all external lights and lamp fixtures.

❏ Superior Industries International Inc.: wheels.

❏ Benteler Automotive Corp.: rear suspension.

❏ Draftex: sealing systems and weatherstripping. ❏

chapter 3

PUTTING IT TOGETHER

Assembly of the new Thunderbird takes place in Ford Motor Co.'s plant in Wixom, Michigan, 25 miles northwest of Dearborn. Wixom originally built 1958 Thunderbirds and Lincolns. It's currently where the new Lincoln LS, Continental and Town Car are assembled.

All 2002 T-Birds come to life in an area of the huge

Assemblers inspect their handiwork at the end of the Wixom line after putting together a pre-production 2002 Thunderbird. This was part of an early exercise to check out assembly procedures and ensure that everything fit properly.

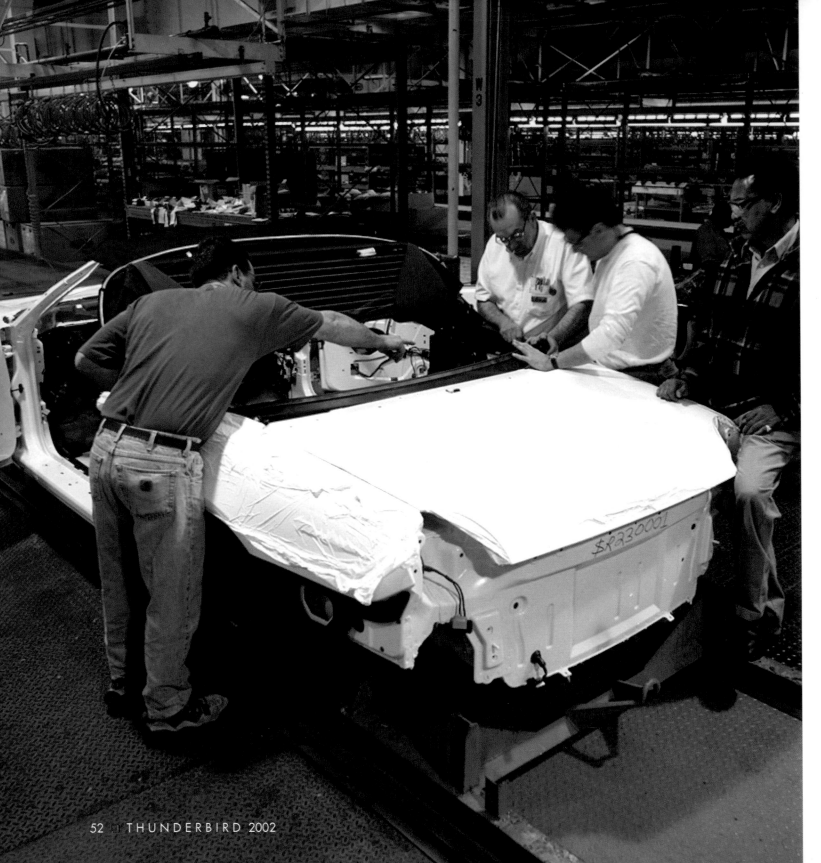

Wixom plant where the Lincoln Mark VIII used to be put together. The 2002 Thunderbird body is assembled on unique tooling within the Wixom bodyshop facility, although paint and sealing operations take place alongside the Lincoln assembly lines.

Let's say you're a visitor to the Wixom plant, and you're there to watch the birth of one particular Thunderbird. You walk along beside it as this car moves from station to station. In following alongside, you note, first of all, that many of the assembly processes are carried out by hand, not by robots or machines. This in itself is unusual. Most modern assembly plants tend to be highly automated. But in the quantities Ford projects for the Thunderbird—some 25,000 cars a

Inside the Wixom plant, workmen prepare to assemble Thunderbird pre-production body #01. Shown (l-r) are Mike Tadra, Dick Harrington, Joe Rocco and Carl Shazar.

year—skilled workers do a better job at lower cost than automatons.

You start your tour at an area at one end of the facility called simply "the bodyshop." Here, in its earliest stages, the floor of the car comes together. It's made up of underbody sheetmetal stampings that arrive at the plant from various sources. These are the floor sub-assemblies and, according to Thunderbird vehicle operations launch leader Jim Walesch, "The underbody is itself made up of a number of subassemblies—a front structure, a front floorpan, a center pan and a rear pan. Each of these is likewise made up of subassemblies within themselves. They all go into an underbody marriage fixture and are welded together. You then have this basic platform that the sides and back panels of the body attach to."

Assemblers position convertible top mechanism with an overhead crane. Bodysides are protected with a plastic film.

The finished floorpan moves into the body framing fixture, where the body sides, lower and upper back panels and windshield header are welded in place. Special holding fixtures guarantee the precise alignment of all these sheetmetal components. The structure now starts to look a little like a car.

As the evolving car moves along on skids atop a conveyor, small teams of workers continually add parts, and there's the ever-present sputter and crackle of electric arc welders. Orange sparks fly in all directions.

You've now reached the area of the bodyshop where "body closures" are installed. These are the items that open and close: doors, hood and decklid. A small work team pre-assembles the door hinges to the doors. The doors are then loaded into fixtures that locate them to the body. These fixtures hold the doors in place while the workers bolt on the hinges.

After the doors are attached, the vehicle moves to another station where a team

installs the front fenders, hood and decklid. Special fixturing again holds these large SMC panels in position to line them up before their respective bolts get snugged down. The workers use handtools, most of which are electrically or pneumatically driven and pre-set to specific torque ratings. That way, nuts and bolts are tightened precisely to specification.

At this point, the basic body is essentially done. Before it moves

Kristine Horvath tightens top framework, assisted by Mark Schooder and Jay Haubenstrickler.

into the next major area, paint, it's carefully inspected. Welds receive the eagle eye, and expert metal finishers look for tiny dings and imperfections in the sheetmetal. The fits of doors, the hood and fenders get checked and adjusted. These are craftsmen who, if they find even a

scratch or the slightest ripple, do whatever is necessary to get everything perfect before painting. "This is an important step," says Walesch, "toward getting an ultra-high-quality vehicle."

In the paint area—and you can watch the action through large windows—the body is first thoroughly cleaned with a phosphate solution. It's then totally submerged in a huge tank filled with "E-coat." The term E-coat is short for electrophoretic deposit of polymers. Basically it's a chemical solution that's allowed to seep and gurgle into the body's every nook and cranny, no matter how hidden. The E-coat's main purpose is to prevent rusting in the car's later life.

Once the body comes out of the E-coat, it's heat-dried, after which seam sealers are applied. The sealers are put on partly with hand-held sprayers and partly with robot guns. Notes Jim Walesch, "The sealer application for other cars built at Wixom is far more automated than the Thunderbird's, because the Bird body has some hard-to-reach places, especially where the con-

vertible top attaches. This keeps the sealer from getting up into the inner surfaces of the wheelhouses, for example. We use manual processes for areas not accessible to robots."

After the sealer comes a robotically applied primer coat. The primer coat is then baked. Next comes a base coat of actual paint, also robotically applied. This base coat contains the color of the car. The base coat is surprisingly thin—only a few microns deep—and it looks fairly lusterless, with a definite matte surface finish.

Finally, a clear coat is robotically sprayed over the base coat. This immediately makes the car look like someone splashed water all over it. The vehicle is then baked in ovens, which hardens the clear coat over the colored base and, instead of looking dull, the final finish now looks bright and glossy and about two feet deep.

❏ ONWARD AND UPWARD
The entire painting process takes about six hours, after which the body is transferred to an elevator and taken up to the trim department

on the second floor, where the final assembly operations take place. In "trim," the first job is to install the wiring harnesses. The Thunderbird, as mentioned in Chapter Two, needs less actual wire than most cars of this size, thanks to multiplexing. Wiring is done entirely by hand, the wires and their connectors are color coded to make assembly easier.

Next process in the trim area is to install the folding convertible top. This takes a certain amount of skill, but the work team makes the task look effortless. One worker attaches the Thunderbird logos to the rear quarters and decklid, and another attaches the outer door handles and external mirrors, bolting them in place from inside the doors.

As the car travels down the line, the heater and air-conditioner evaporator are installed, with ducting and hoses routed in seemingly random directions. And the wind-

Mike Wehr checks mechanical details on another pre-production Thunderbird.

shield wiper module gets tucked up into the cowl, the carpeting gets put in, followed by the floor console, which fits like a long cap over the driveshaft tunnel. Workers then install the shift selector lever. Once the behind-dash and under-cowl hardware is installed. next comes

the instrument panel itself, a sub-assembly complete with gauges, center stack, wiring, bulbs, vents, steering wheel and airbags.

Then into the doors go the glass, electric window-lift motors, speakers and the door trim panels. This is followed by the installation of

kick panels and trim for the rear compartment, around the windshield, etc. The windshield glass comes down, held by big suction cups on a special jig, and gets positioned, cemented and trimmed. An electrical inspection makes sure all the wires are connected. The paint-

Black Bird gets a final going over from (l-r) Steve Hegberg, Mark Jarosz, Rick Walters and Bill Viers. Pre-production cars were put to many uses, including testing and advertising photography.

ed, trimmed body is now ready to head back down on another elevator to continue the final operations.

❑ AND DOWN TO EARTH AGAIN
Back on the main floor, the body moves along on pallets and special rails. It's sometimes at shoulder height, because this is where the mechanical components will be added, most of them from below.

The fuel tank goes in first. At the next station, the body is lowered onto a pallet that contains a number of pre-assembled components, namely the air-conditioning condenser, radiator, engine, transmission, driveshaft, front and rear subframes, axles and suspension systems. Everything gets attached in place, and the car moves along to the next area, where the exhaust system gets bolted up under the chassis.

Next, the front and rear body fascias are installed along with the headlamps. One station farther along, the wheels are bolted on, after which the car is lowered onto a conveyor. It's now rolling on its own tires. As it moves along, a

worker puts the battery in the trunk and connects it. Then come the seats. Color keyed to the car, the seats drop down from an overhead conveyor and are bolted to the floorpan. After that, the radiator, power steering, brakes, windshield washer reservoir and the a/c system are all properly filled.

Finally, at the end of the line, a worker puts gasoline in the fuel tank, another hops into the driver's seat and turns the key. With a wondrous sound, the engine springs to life, the driver drops the shifter into gear and the car moves majestically into the wheel-alignment bay. After the wheels are aligned, the car is driven into the dyno and functional system checking bay, where it's hooked up to a computer that tests the car's onboard electronics.

The computer interfaces with the car's own microprocessors and, in some cases, programs them. It tests the powertrain sensors and the car's central processing unit, the security system, cruise control and the sound system. It adjusts such things as the audio system's speaker and equalizer balance. The comput-

er operator also tests other electrical functions such as headlights, horn, emergency flashers, directional signals, etc. And while these electronic tests are going on, the headlights get aimed and adjusted.

As a final check, the car goes to the water-test facility where, with the cloth top up and all windows tightly shut, it's driven through a long tunnel filled with water sprayers. This tests for leaks. At the end of the tunnel, if any traces of water are found inside the car, a

special team makes adjustments to the windows and top seals and runs the car back through to be sure they've stopped the leaks. Cars with optional removable tops are subjected to a second water test for the same purpose.

After thoroughly drying the exterior of the car, it's parked in a huge lot outside the Wixom plant, ready to be shipped. Within days, it'll be delivered to a Ford dealer, and soon after that, the car will find a home with a lucky new owner. ❑

Pre-introduction Thunderbird ad showed Fairlane-inspired chrome side trim. The striking "Fairlane stripe" appeared on early proto-types but didn't make production.

A fabric top whisks into place in seconds — to protect you from sudden rainstorms. It's completely out of sight when not in use.

Enchantment unlimited...the new Ford THUNDERBIRD

A distinguished kind of personal car that combines high performance and high style for a whole new world of driving fun.

The removable, glass-fibre hard top is easy to handle . . . locks into place to give you winter-long comfort.

Those long, low lines . . . the sweeping, contoured windshield . . . say distinction in every detail.

CAST ASIDE all of your previous ideas of what driving can be like. Here is something so totally fresh that it offers you a completely new concept of all-round driving enjoyment.

The Thunderbird's long, low, thoroughbred lines say "action" in every detail! And they speak the truth.

Your slightest toe-touch on the gas pedal means no waiting.

There's breath-taking Trigger-Torque performance with the new Thunderbird Special V-8 that's specially mated with transmission and rear axle. It's a delightful kind of performance that is unequaled by any other American car.

With a low center of gravity (from cowl to ground is just over three feet) and Ford's Ball-Joint Front Suspension, the Thunderbird corners as if on rails.

The fun doesn't stop here, for the Thunderbird is long on convenience.

Two tops are available. There's a removable glass-fibre hard top . . . and a smart convertible fabric top. Windows roll up. The extra-wide foam-rubber-cushioned seat moves forward or back, up or down, at the touch of a button. The baggage compartment is ample. There's a telescoping steering wheel. And you can have power steering, brakes, and windows . . . Fordomatic or Overdrive.

Why not call on your Ford Dealer today and get complete details on this new and distinctive personal car? First deliveries of the thrilling Thunderbird are now being made.

chapter 4

HERITAGE

In the beginning was the Bird, and the Bird was good. Today, nearly half a century later, the Ford Thunderbird has led many lives, and it's been around the block a few times.

This history begins with a spirited, luxurious two-seater—a thoroughly modern car by the

standards of its day, yet somehow rooted in the past. No one used the word "retro" back in 1954, but that first Thunderbird clearly contained classic styling elements.

Franklin Q. Hershey designed the car that way. As Ford Division's design director from late 1952 until mid 1955, Hershey was the man responsible for the first Thunderbird's creation. Historians sometimes dispute his role, but there's no doubt that the initial idea for the car was his. And he did manage the studio where it was designed.

Hershey was steeped in the classics. He started in 1929 working for the coachbuilder Walter M. Murphy in Pasadena, California. Murphy produced custom automobile bodies for Hollywood's gliterati. When Murphy sold his shop in 1932, Hershey went to General Motors, where he spent the next 20 years designing Pontiacs, Opels and Cadillacs.

Ford hired him in late 1952 to head up its Ford Division design studio. A few months later, a colleague from Chevrolet visited Frank

Classic Thunderbirds did have the ability to attract crowds. This is the 1956 Bird, recognizable by its continental kit and bumper exhaust ports.

The production 1955 Thunderbird in full feather.

at his home and showed him pre-announcement photographs of the Corvette. Frank was shocked that Chevrolet was working on so sleek and radical a two-seater, and he decided that Ford needed a response. He immediately asked two designers in his studio—Bill Boyer and Damon Woods—to come up with Ford's answer to the Corvette.

Under Hershey's guidance, the emerging two-seater took on a lot of the classic elements from his Murphy days: the simple, graceful, horizontal sweep from front to rear, the reverse-wedge profile, the long hood and short deck, the snug top and wraparound dash sill.

At first, Hershey and his staff worked on the two-seater in secret. No one outside the studio knew about it. Then, little by little, word leaked out. Finally Ford's engineering vice president, Earle S. MacPherson, heard what was happening and ordered Hershey to shut the project down. Hershey threw a cloth over the full-sized clay model and put it in a corner of the studio.

It was about then, in October 1952, that Henry Ford II and Ford's design consultant, George W. Walker, toured the Paris auto show together. Henry Ford II liked sports cars and got all excited about the Jaguars and Ferraris on

display. According to a cover article in *Time* magazine, Henry Ford II asked Walker, "Why can't we build a car like that?" Whereupon Walker, aware of Hershey's clandestine two-seater, said that he already had one in the works. Walker, so goes the story, then slipped into a phone booth and called Dearborn. He asked that Hershey's clay model be ready for review by the time Walker and Henry Ford II returned. The informal walk-around, which included Ford Division general manager Lewis D. (Lew) Crusoe, got everyone excited, but no one suggested that Ford actually build such a car.

❏ AN IDEA TAKES WING
Lew Crusoe, like Henry Ford II, also took an interest in European sports cars, not so much as an enthusiast but as a businessman watching the British sell roadsters here. By examining the market, Crusoe discovered an open niche for a two-seater priced just below Jaguar's XK-120.

So Crusoe and Hershey seemed to be moving in the same direction—toward an attractive, high-spirited, two-place convertible in the tradition of classic speedsters like the Auburn and Packard boat-tails. Hershey's interpretation of this concept would become, as Ford product-planning chief Chase Morsey called it, a "personal car." Years later, Hershey said that the car he had in mind "was one a bank president...could drive with-out...having people point and say, 'Look who thinks he's still a kid.'"

Thirty days after General Motors unveiled the Corvette, Ford approved Hershey's two-seater. The official date was 9 February 1953. As it progressed, Hershey's clay model borrowed design cues from both the '55 Ford sedan and the evolving '56 Continental Mark II.

The new car didn't have a name, so Ford's ad agency, J. Walter Thompson, made a list of some 5000 possibilities. The candidates included Fordster, Fordette, Beaver, Detroiter, Hep Cat and Wheelaway. Fortunately, Lew Crusoe didn't like any of those names, and he offered a prize—a $250 suit—to any Ford employee who could come up with a better

The porthole top initially appeared on the 1956 Thunderbird. And the most famous use of the porthole was by George Lucas in *American Grafitti* when a mysterious Suzanne Somers beckons Richard Dreyfuss.

one. A young designer, Alden R. (Gib) Giberson, who'd lived in the southwest, suggested *Thunderbird*, borrowing the name from Native American lore. Crusoe immediately accepted it, and Gib got his suit.

❏ PUBLIC GOT FIRST PEEK IN '54
The production car would have a ground clearance of 5.5 inches and stand a mere 36 inches high at the cowl, extremely low even now. Its 102-inch wheelbase was the same as the Corvette's and the Jaguar XK-120's. The XK-120 was the car Hershey used to benchmark his Thunderbird's seating position, steering-wheel angle and interior dimensions. Like the Jaguar, the original Thunderbird's seats stood just ahead of the rear wheels, allowing the engine to be positioned behind the front-axle centerline. This made for more equal weight distribution which, in turn, gave better handling and lighter steering.

The Thunderbird's basic packaging was worked out by Ford Division's chief engineer, Bill Burnett. Burnett literally cut up a 1953 Ford sedan and welded it back together

to approximate the two-seater's proportions and weight distribution. Toad ugly with its exposed welds, the prototype was labeled "Burnetti" by members of Ford Division's engineering staff (see last page).

One requirement of the first Thunderbird was that it share as many parts as possible with Ford sedans and wagons. The Bird's frame had to be unique, and it consisted of box-section side rails with a central X-member. The 292-cubic-inch-displacement (cid) V8, though, was basically the same as in Ford and Mercury passenger cars. With its four-barrel carburetor and dual exhausts, the 1955 Thunderbird 292 produced 193 brake horse-power (bhp) in manual-shift models and 198 bhp with the automatic transmission. To tuck the engine under the low hood, designer Dave Ash came up with a neat little scoop to clear the air cleaner.

A wooden mockup of the Thunderbird, realistic in every detail, was shown to the public at the Detroit Auto Show in February 1954. Production started on 9 September 1954, and the

Thunderbird went on sale on 22 October. Its base price, $2944, made it the most expensive Ford available. Standard equipment included a clock and tachometer, removable hardtop, adjustable steering column and a four-way power seat. A disappearing cloth top, power steering, power brakes, overdrive and automatic transmission were all available at extra cost. Most T-Bird buyers loaded their cars with options, which pushed the selling price into Lincoln territory, around $3500. That first model year, Ford planners calculated that dealers would sell approximately 10,000 Thunderbirds in all. By early November, though, some 3500 orders had already come flooding in, and by the end of the 1955 model year, Ford had sold 16,155 Thunderbirds.

A few design glitches showed up in the '55s. Crusoe himself complained of poor ventilation and blind spots with the hardtop. So for 1956, the Thunderbird came with cowl side vents and a set of windwings. To address the second problem, Ford designed a new top.

The 1957 Thunderbird sprouted tailfins, kept the porthole top but shed the continental spare tire. This final year of the two-seater saw versions of the 312-cubic-inch V8 that produced up to 300 horsepower with the addition of a McCulloch supercharger.

Early renditions had quarter panes behind the regular windows. The rear panes were hard to seal, though, and in May 1955, someone suggested a nautical solution: portholes. Portholes required no change to the 1955's weather stripping and cost less to produce than quarter panes. Ford offered the porthole top as a no-cost option on 1956-57 Thunderbirds, and 80% of all buyers chose it over the blind-quarter roof.

To make more room in the trunk, the 1956 Bird got a continental kit. The external spare meant moving the dual exhausts to the corners of the rear bumper, and it also changed the car's weight distribution from 52/48 to 49/51. This, in turn, necessitated engineering revisions throughout the car. The frame was reinforced, the suspension re-tuned and the steering re-geared, all to compensate for the weight of the rear spare. An optional 312-cid, 225 bhp V8 for 1956 kept acceleration about the same as in 1955.

In 1956, too, Ford bravely launched a safety campaign. The Thunderbird, along with full-sized Fords, offered a padded dashboard

The 1958 T-Bird, right, kept many of the '57's styling cues, including the simplified grille and hood scoop, but added quad headlamps and rockets on the rear quarter panels.

The four-place 1958 Bird was one of the first U.S. production cars to offer bucket seats and console. Its extremely low floor resulted from the "cowbelly" frame integrated into unitized body construction.

padded sunvisors, deep-dish steering wheel and optional seatbelts.

For the two-seater's final year, 1957, Ford designer Rhys Miller lengthened the trunk (no more outside spare), enlarged the fins and put on a bigger bumper/grille. These changes kept the Thunderbird's styling in line with the full-sized '57 Ford.

The Bird's 312 V8 now produced 245 bhp, and a twin-four-barrel version, known as the E-Bird (its serial number started with "E"), delivered 270 to 285 bhp. Meanwhile, the even hotter 1957 F-Birds delivered 300 bhp thanks to a McCulloch centrifugal supercharger. The '57 model was not only the fastest of the two-seater Birds but also the most popular, with 21,380 built during a slightly extended selling season. It would also be the last two-seater Thunderbird for 44 years.

❏ TWO PLUS TWO MAKES FOUR

In January 1955, Robert F. McNamara, one of the original Whiz Kids who'd saved the company after World War II, became Ford Division's new general manager,

In an effort to bring back a two-seater, Ford created the 1962 Thunderbird Sports Roadster by putting a fiberglass tonneau over the rear seats.

replacing Lew Crusoe. McNamara, a consummate beancounter, decided—rightly—that what the future Thunderbird needed was two more seats. Frank Hershey pleaded with McNamara to keep the two-seater in production alongside the four-seater,

but McNamara vetoed that idea.

The four-place Thunderbird became official on 9 March 1955. The new car would use what Dearborn engineers called the "cowbelly" frame. In this, the two main rails bowed outward on both sides,

and the floor hung off the bottom. That way, the entire car could stand lower. Ford first used the cowbelly perimeter frame under the 1956-57 Continental Mark II, and now Ford's body engineers were anxious to take the next step and integrate it into the

body itself. Unibody construction would lower the '58 Thunderbird's profile yet give lots of interior space.

Ford had already built a new plant in Wixom, Michigan, purely for unibody construction. By early 1956, Ford executives had decided to switch the entire 1958 Lincoln and Continental lines to uni-body construction, and now the Thunderbird would be built at Wixom as well. The idea was to assure higher quality for all FoMoCo premium automobiles.

In May 1955, Henry Ford II named George Walker as the company's first vice president of design. Frank Hershey resigned, and Bill Boyer was now put in charge of the Thunderbird studio under Walker's lieutenant, Joe Oros. Many of the '58 Thunderbird's wildest styling features, including its dual-pod rear end, had been worked out on early '58 two-seater sketches.

❑ THE SQUAREBIRD ARRIVES
Despite its rear seats, the '58 Thunderbird coupe stood just one inch taller than the '57 hardtop and 3.7 inches lower than a '58 full-sized Ford, yet it offered virtually the same headroom and ground clearance. To accomplish this, Thunderbird passengers sat very deep within the car, down between the wide door sills and massive center tunnel. Cleverly, Boyer turned a

problem into an asset by decking out the tunnel as a full-length console. Front bucket seats, never offered in the two-seater, were standard on the 1958 "Squarebird," as it came to be called. GM had previously fielded a few four-place show-cars with bucket seats and full-length consoles, but Ford put the idea into production.

The only Thunderbird engine offered in '58 was a 300-bhp, 352-cid V8. The Squarebird's proportions still allowed the engine to sit well back in the chassis, for a 50/50

Bullet-shaped silhouette of the 1961 Thunderbird remained virtually unchanged for 1962-63.

The 1963 Bird is identifiable by a feature line along the side, with three hashmarks on the door.

Luxurious 1963 leather interior featured SwingAway steering column, full-length console, coved rear seat and an abundance of chrome and aluminum trim.

weight distribution. And, with its low center of gravity and 113-inch wheelbase, the Squarebird was a decent handler despite relatively soft coil springs all around. The fixed-hardtop version appeared in January 1958, followed by a convertible in June. The convertible, a minor engineering marvel, flipped its soft top into the front-opening trunk with the flick of a switch. With the top down, there wasn't much room for luggage, but the top was totally hidden. Ford sold 37,892 four-seaters for 1958.

Only minor changes appeared for 1959 and '60, largely because the '58 had cost $40 million to develop and Ford management wasn't anxious to invest much more. There were grille and trim changes, and the 1959 Bird reverted to rear leaf springs. It also added the mighty 430-cid, 350-bhp Lincoln V8 as an option. Thus equipped, the Thunderbird could do 0-100 mph in just 24 seconds. And in 1959 alone, Ford sold 67,456 Thunderbirds, more than all three years of two-seater combined.

In 1960, Henry Ford II became company chairman, McNamara succeeded him as president, and that put Lido A. (Lee) Iacocca, 35, in the top office at Ford Division. Marketing whiz Iacocca would soon make a name for himself with the 1965 Mustang.

For 1960, the Thunderbird offered a sliding steel sunroof. It added $212 to the coupe's $3755 price, and 2536 sunroofs were sold. Otherwise, revised tail lamps and grille changes distinguished the '60 Bird from 1958-59 models. Ford sold 92,843 Thunderbirds that season, a record that would stand for 16 years. And every personal car built since 1958, from the Buick Riviera to the BMW 850i, owes its existence to Mr. McNamara and his trendsetting 1958 Thunderbird. The Squarebird of 1958-60 was even more original, successful and oft-copied than even the more fondly remembered Early Bird of 1955-57.

Yet the Squarebird was also the last of its kind—the last Thunderbird that could be ordered as a high-zoot hot rod, with non-power steering, manual floorshift and overdrive. Of course, very few

Dealers offered Sports Roadster tonneaus for the totally restyled 1964 Thunderbird.

were ever built that way. Most T-Bird buyers opted for automatic transmissions and every conceivable power accessory. So the 1961 Thunderbird came only with a 390-cid V8, automatic, power steering and brakes—everything included in its $4170 base price. And the T-Bird's role as a stylish but mature luxury coupe now became more clearly defined.

Almost as radically changed as in '58, the 1961 Thunderbird shared little more than its 113-inch wheelbase with its predecessor. Front track was widened an inch, rear track by three. The front still rode on coil springs, but a lateral arm and tension strut replaced the lower wishbone, decreasing ride harshness without softening the spring rate.

Even the unit body was all-new, with more interior room, a lower tunnel and wider opening doors. The steering ratio was faster, the brakes stronger. The steering wheel was smaller, and it swung to the right on a hidden track, making it easier for the driver to get in and out. (Optional in '61, this popular feature became standard in '62.) Horsepower remained at 300, but torque rose from 381 to 427 ft. lb. at 2800 rpm. Yet sales sank to a disappointing 73,051.

The contemporary press laid the blame on the Bird's controversial new styling. As *Motor Trend* noted in December 1960, "People seem to like it very much or not at all; few express an opinion in between the two extremes."

Oros, Boyer and Woods had enthusiastically sculpted the new

rocketship design, with its gently rounded sides, integrated bumper/grille and what Elwood Engel called "flower-pot" tail lights. Engel himself, a Walker veteran who supervised the Lincoln-Mercury studio, had developed an alternative Thunderbird proposal, with very clean slab sides, square corners and a distinct razor-edged chrome molding that topped the beltline on either side, running from the front bumper to the rear. Walker openly favored the so-called "Engelbird," while McNamara thought Engel's car could be stretched and made into the 1961 Lincoln Continental. When Henry Ford II asked Oros, in front of the dissenting Walker, which model he preferred, Oros bravely defended his own design as "racy, purposeful and more apropos to a sporty car." Ford said nothing at the time, but McNamara got his new Lincoln Continental, and Oros got his racy Thunderbird, albeit modified with Engel's razor-edge fenders. Oros later allowed that having similar fender forms on the two cars simplified assembly at Wixom. The '61 Thunderbird and Continental also featured Ford's first curved side glass.

❏ ENTER THE SPORTS ROADSTER

Nineteen sixty-two brought minor styling revisions: a checkerboard grille, simplified hood and side trim that emphasized the car's length. A high-performance engine option returned, and two new body styles were added. The "M-Series" 390 V8 used the better-breathing, higher-compression heads from the Ford 406 plus triple carburetors to boost horsepower to 340 at 5000 rpm.

Despite the success of four-place Thunderbirds, people still felt a certain longing for the two-seater. At one point, Iacocca suggested to product planner Tom Case to consider reviving the 1957 Bird. Budd still had the body dies, so maybe Ford could build a two-seater on the Falcon platform. Budd did fabricate a single prototype, the XT-Bird, but by then Iacocca and Case were busy with the Mustang.

The closest Iacocca came to a two-seater was the 1962 Thunderbird Sports Roadster. This simulated a two-seater by hiding the rear seat under a fiberglass tonneau. Sports Roadsters came with Kelsey-Hayes chrome wire wheels, but an unimpressed public ordered only 1427 during the '62 model year.

More popular was the new

Landau model, essentially a standard hardtop with a padded vinyl roof (still something of a novelty then) and S-shaped landau irons on its broad, flat B-pillars. The Landau would survive as a Thunderbird variant through 1971. Total Bird sales for 1962 inched up encouragingly to 78,011. Maybe buyers needed time to get used to the rocket look. Or perhaps the Sports Roadster and M-engine had helped promote the Thunderbird after all.

The facelifted 1963 Thunderbird looked a bit more formal, and the Sports Roadster continued to limp along. Only 455 got sold that year, 37 of them with M-engines. Thunderbird sales for 1963 slipped to 63,313, but that actually wasn't bad because, for the first time ever, the four-seater T-Bird had competition. Buick's all-new 1963 Riviera attracted some 40,000 buyers, so the Bird, with a three-year-old design, could take some pride in staying better than 50% ahead.

Completely restyled for '64—square-edged and sharply creased—the new Bird built on the

1961-63 rocketship look while blending in some of the rectangular shapes from 1958-60. A return to flat side glass emphasized the sheer form of the greenhouse. Interior styling was completely new also, with a futuristic dash design, flow-through ventilation and a neat wrap-around cove effect for the rear seat. The public loved this car, as evidenced by 82,865 sales.

Mechanical changes, however, were minimal. The M-series V8 was gone, so once again the 300-bhp 390 became the only available engine. And for its final year, Ford redesigned the 1964 Sports Roadster tonneau and made it optional only as a dealer add-on. Nineteen sixty-five brought front disc brakes and triple turn signals that flashed in sequence like a Las Vegas marquee. For '66, the designers

"Knudsen nose" graced 1970 Thunderbird. Insurance companies disliked prow grille, because it tended to get crunched in parking maneuvers.

scrapped the Bird's integrated bumper/grille in favor of a mesh air inlet intersected by a thin blade bumper. Out back, the sequential tail lights merged to form a single unit stretching, wall to wall, all the way across the rear.

The new Town Landau, with its blind-quarter roof, was the Bird's bestselling body style by far; but there were also blind-but-painted Town Hardtops and just plain Hardtops with quarter windows—

plus the final Thunderbird convertible, which sold 5049 copies. Under the hood, the 390 V8 now rated 315 bhp, and an optional 428-cid V8 delivered 345 horses at 4600 rpm. Bigger changes were on their way for 1967, because the personal luxury market, once exclusive to the Thunderbird, now began to get crowded.

By 1966, Thunderbird competitors included the elegant, second-generation Riviera; the trendset-

Thunderbirds shared the Lincoln Continental's body shell for 1972. Opera window was added in '73, and during 1974-76, only the 460 V8 was available.

ting, front-wheel-drive Oldsmobile Toronado; and it was known that Cadillac would introduce a new Eldorado for 1967. All three GM coupes were bigger and costlier

than the Thunderbird, but the Bird still led in sales. Ford wanted to keep it that way.

With a wheelbase of 114.7 inches, the all-new 1967 model

Large, heavy and luxurious, the 1975 Bird offered optional four-wheel disc brakes with antilock rears.

became the largest Thunderbird ever. And for the first time, the line included a four-door sedan as well as the coupe. The sedan rode on a 117.2-inch wheelbase and had front-opening rear doors, like the Lincoln Continental. Both T-Bird body styles came with bucket seats, a sweeping console, and two-door models had coved rear seats.

The extensively re-engineered '67 Thunderbird was no longer unibodied. The new, "rigidized" body mounted at four points to a separate, relatively compliant frame. The body mounts were located where the frame moved the least, a configuration that minimized noise, vibration and harshness. And while body-on-frame vehicles usually weigh more than their unitized equivalents, in this case a two-door 1967 T-Bird actually weighed 138 pounds less than its unibodied predecessor. Front and rear frame sections, incidentally, were shared with the big Ford, as was the Bird's all-coil suspension system.

Engine choices remained the same, with the 315-bhp 390 V8 standard and the 345-horse 428 as

an option. But even that changed in 1968, when the new, super-duty 429 replaced the 428. The 429 became standard at mid year.

Inside, the 1968 Thunderbird offered a bench front seat for the first time since 1957. General Motors' personal cars all offered bench seating, and benches were clearly what the public preferred that year. Only 57% of two-door Bird buyers opted for bucket seats, while 79% of four-door buyers chose benches.

But was a four-door Thunderbird sedan still a personal car? That question vexed Ford's new CEO, Semon E. (Bunkie) Knudsen, who'd been lured away from General Motors in early 1968. Knudsen felt that the Thunderbird might be growing too large, too soft and too conventional. The Pontiac Grand Prix had wandered into a similar dilemma, and Knudsen knew that the 1969 Grand Prix would use General Motors' smaller mid-sized body shell with a stretched hood. This gave the Grand Prix good proportions but kept size and weight reasonable.

Knudsen believed a comparable approach might work for the Thunderbird and encouraged the development of a new Bird based on the next generation of Ford's intermediates. The designers and engineers were then developing all-new mid-sized cars for 1970, using the same nodal-point, body-on-frame construction as the full-sized Fords.

In the meantime, there was not much Bunkie could do about the '69 models. Suspension revisions hunkered the T-Bird down lower on its wheels, and two-doors now had firmer spring rates than four-doors. The blind quarter Landau returned after a two-year absence and outsold conventional hardtops and four-doors combined. Two-door Landaus alone could be equipped with an electric sunroof.

In 1969, the Buick Riviera outsold the Thunderbird for the first time: 52,872 to 49,272. And Pontiac sold an impressive 112,486 Grands Prix. Henry Ford II sacked Bunkie in September, after Knudsen and Iacocca clashed. Meanwhile, Ford's new intermediates got delayed until 1972.

Still, Bunkie did affect the styling of the 1970 Thunderbird, with its lower, longer roof and the infamous "Knudsen nose." The Knudsen nose offered virtually no bumper protection and became an insurer's nightmare. The T-Bird's suspension was re-tuned for radial tires, and the car now shared the premium sound insulation package from the mechanically similar Continental Mark III. The blind-quarter Landau went away again, then returned for 1971 and once more outsold all other body styles combined. Sales of the four-door model dropped off after 1969, and 1971 would be its last year.

When the mid-sized 1972 Thunderbird finally did arrive, with its wheelbase stretched to 120 inches, it looked even bigger than the full-sized Bird it replaced. Overall length was reduced by only an inch, but weight—at 4420 pounds—was slightly higher. Sales rebounded to 57,814 for the Bird's best showing since 1968.

A 1973 facelift put more chrome on the front and Continental-style opera windows in

In 1977, downsized T-Bird became a Ford LTD II clone, with a 302 V8 standard. Next year would see 352,751 Thunderbirds sold, more than ever before or since.

For 1979, optional T-top cost $747, and the CB radio—a $295 extra—was all the rage.

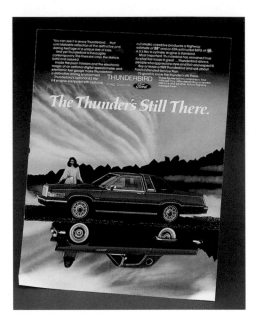

Downsizing the 1980 Thunderbird on Ford's Fox platform made the marque thriftier, easier to drive and park. At right, check out the car reflected in the puddle. Ford was cashing in on T-Bird's heritage even in those days.

the roof sail panels. It was a boom year for the industry, and the Bird scored 87,269 sales, the highest figure since '64. After 1973, though, fuel crunches, inflation and a tightening economy cut into the market for large, heavy cars. Ford downsized the Mustang for 1974, and the Mustang immediately took off. But the mid-sized Bird was caught in a time warp, and by 1976, sales fell to 36,578.

❏ SLIMMER AND TRIMMER
While the intermediate T-Bird held its own against full-sized competitors like the Riviera and Eldorado, it couldn't stop GM's trimmer mid-

sized personal cars. These included the Pontiac Grand Prix and now the budget-priced Chevrolet Monte Carlo. With Ford's own mid-sized lineup due for a makeover in '77, Dearborn decided to trim the Thunderbird down to true intermediate proportions, on a wheelbase of just 114 inches. The standard engine would be a 130-bhp small-block 302 V8 (horsepower ratings were now net instead of gross), with a 149-bhp 351 and 173-horse 400 V8s as options.

Sensible as it sounds, the decision presented Ford's design studios with a serious challenge: If the Thunderbird shared dimensions

with the garden-variety, mid-sized Ford LTD II hardtop—not to mention several Mercurys—how could it hold on to its distinctive personality?

Fortunately, the mid-size program was headed by Gale Halderman, a veteran designer who'd worked on every Thunderbird since the 1958 model. Breaking with tradition, Halderman's studio devised a thin-pillared roof with big rear quarter windows, seemingly strapped down by a sheetmetal band that swept up from behind each door and over the top of the car. Small, vertical windows set into this "basket handle" added more visual interest than outward vision,

but the overall effect of the '77 T-Bird's roof was striking.

The Thunderbird's sheer lower body panels did resemble the Ford LTD II's, but there was no mistaking one car for the other. Alongside the neo-classic Grand Prix and Monte Carlo, the Thunderbird looked slim, modern and unmistakably Ford. Sales soared to 318,140, a record by a huge margin. The 1978 T-Bird, only mildly revised, sold 352,751, which still stands as its record sales year.

But like the two-seater before it, the basket-handle Bird was doomed from the start. To meet federal Corporate Average Fuel

Economy (CAFE) regulations, Ford would have to downsize the Thunderbird, as it had the Mustang. The company did this by putting the 1980 model on the unitized "Fox" platform, which it shared with the 1978 Ford Fairmont and the 1979 Mustang, among others.

In hindsight, the 1980-82 Thunderbird became something of an engineering achievement: bigger on the inside, better handling than before and so much lighter that the 302 V8 delivered nearly the same acceleration numbers as the 400 had in 1977-78. Economy-minded buyers could choose a 255-cid V8; a 200-cid, in-line Six (after spring 1980); or even a 232-cid (3.8-liter) V6 in '82. But many people didn't like the Fox Bird's styling and, after three years, sales decreased to a disappointing 45,142.

By then, though, an entirely new management team was running Dearborn. In 1979, Philip Caldwell, the previous head of Ford's overseas operations, succeeded the retiring Henry Ford II as chairman. In March 1980, Caldwell installed product planner Don Petersen in the presi-dent's office, and Jack Telnack was now in charge of mid-sized car design, including the Thunderbird.

Telnack's first concern, how-ever, was the delicate downsizing of the luxurious Lincoln, a process that hadn't been going well. As an experiment, he assigned designers Allen Ornes and John Aiken to work out a new Mark VII coupe on a stretched Fox platform. True stream-lining was an inexpensive, practical way to improve fuel economy, so Ornes and Aiken created a stun-ningly aerodynamic shape for the Lincoln Mark VII, which Petersen heartily endorsed.

❏ BORN IN THE WINDTUNNEL
Feeling that the Thunderbird, too, needed a fresh start, the same group, along with Halderman, adopted a similar aerodynamic strategy for Ford's personal car. The streamlined 1983 "Aerobird" went into production one full year ahead of the Lincoln that had given it form.

Mechanically, the Aerobird still used the Fox platform. Wheelbase got cut to 104 inches, which sacrificed some rear-seat leg

Aerobird of 1983 shared Continental Mark VII body shell, laid stylistic groundwork for Ford Taurus/Sable.

Final rear-drive coupe arrived for 1989. This is the 1993 model.

The last Thunderbird coupe bowed out after 1997.

room, yet the coupe remained a full four seater despite the shortest chassis since the two-place original. Initially, the Aerobird offered only the 3.8-liter V6, but the 302 V8 returned in the spring. At the same time, Ford launched the 1983 Thunderbird Turbo Coupe, the first four-cylinder Thunderbird ever produced and the first Bird since 1960 to offer a manual transmission.

But this was no austerity model. With turbocharging and fuel injection, the 2.3-liter, overhead-cam Four delivered 145 bhp. A close-ratio five-speed gearbox, stiffer springs and gas shocks came standard, and *Car and Driver* clocked the Turbo Coupe at 128 mph. For 1987, an intercooler was added, boosting horsepower to 190. Extensive styling changes for all Thunderbirds that year included flush-mounted glass all around.

Public response to the Aerobird was instant and positive. Sales nearly tripled in 1983, to 121,999, then 170,533 in 1984 and leveled off to around 150,000 cars annually in 1985-88. Turbo Coupes represented only a fraction

of sales at first but generated quite a lot of enthusiastic press coverage.

During this same period, Ford launched the aerodynamic Taurus and Sable. Dearborn had committed itself to a new era of aero shapes, firmer handling and a more customer-driven design philosophy. It was in this highly charged atmosphere that planning took root for an all-new 1989 Thunderbird.

The new rear-drive T-Bird's wheelbase went out to 113 inches, yet the new car stood slightly shorter and narrower than the already compact Aerobird. The restyled body appeared tightly wrapped around its wheels, with clean, simple lines and enormous windows. The front suspension reverted to a smooth-riding tension-strut arrangement, used in one form or another from 1961 to 1979. And now, for the first time, the Thunderbird got an independent rear suspension system.

The 3.8-liter V6 returned as the base engine, but the four-cylinder Turbo Coupe gave way to a V6 Super Coupe, which used an Eaton supercharger to pump horsepower up to 210 and torque to 315 ft. lb.

The Super Coupe's electronically controlled suspension was uncompromisingly tight, and the car's performance was nothing short of awesome. Responding to market demand, Ford added a 302 V8 model in '91, a V8-powered Sport edition in '92 and finally the "modular" 4.6-liter, quadcam V8 in '94.

But in the end, the 1989-97 Thunderbird missed its target. Its price bumped heads with the Mustang and, unlike the Mustang, the Thunderbird coupe shared precious little with any of Ford's other cars. So when the coupe market faltered in the mid-1990s, Ford could not justify keeping the Thunderbird in production. As total sales slipped to 79,721 in 1996 and the Super Coupe expired, Ford phased out the Thunderbird altogether at the end of model-year 1997.

The Thunderbird had survived 10 major restylings, three times that many facelifts, had gone from carrying two people to four, then six and finally back to five. And now, after 42 years and 4.2 million automobiles, Ford decided to temporarily fold the Bird's wings. ❑

The 1989-97 Thunderbird carried its driver and passengers in great comfort and style.

chapter 5

ICONOGRAPHY

Because the Ford Thunderbird has become such an American icon, it's firmly embedded in a subculture of collectors. Some people collect the cars themselves, others collect Thunderbird memorabilia, still others track the role of the Bird in time and place.

The 1955-57 Thunderbird surely ranks as one of the most widely recognized of American

Seems fitting that Minnie and Mickey, being icons themselves, should ride in one of America's premier automotive icons, a two-place Thunderbird. Made by Schmid, they're represented here as a ceramic Christmas-tree ornament.

automobiles. It's a symbol of entrepreneurial success, of what we tend to remember of a more innocent, carefree decade. Thunderbird ads from the 1950s and early '60s reinforce that notion.

According to Steve Legel, a Michigan dentist who collects T-Bird memorabilia and related items, Thunderbirds appeared in ads not only for the car but also for auto parts suppliers Bendix and Borg-Warner, for Champion spark plugs, the Budd Co., Cutex nail polish, Monsanto chemicals and Gulf oil.

Actual Thunderbirds, according to Dr. Legel, were given away in 1956 promotions by Karo syrup and Dreft detergent; also by Monsanto in 1957. Clothing manufacturers Arrow and Clipper offered lines of Thunderbird apparel, although no image of the car appeared on them. Fashion ads in *Seventeen* magazine in 1956 featured teenaged girls gathered around a new Thunderbird. Wortex made a Thunderbird jacket, with or without an embroidered T-Bird logo.

In more recent years, classic two-seater Thunderbirds have ap-

Thunderbird iconography comes in all shapes and sizes. At left are tin pencil boxes by the Beetland Co. To the right, Mickey drives a ceramic Thunderbird soap dish. And below is a mechanical bank depicting a T-Bird in a drive-in restaurant. The bank was issued in 1992 by the Franklin Mint.

peared in advertisements for Peerless faucets and have been given away as prizes in the Colorado, California and Idaho state lotteries. Thunderbirds have appeared on bottles of Avon's aftershave and cologne for men. Penney's, Steinmart and Scrubs all offer Hawaiian shirts with pictures of Thunderbirds. And at least four different Thunderbird-print materials are available in fabric stores.

Miss Piggy and Kermit the Frog, both dressed in driving togs, take a spin in their ceramic 1957 Thunderbirds.

Above, Corgi Classics Ltd. of Great Britain made sure that Elvis remains every bit as immortal as the classic Thunderbird. At right, whimsical salt and pepper shakers again capitalize on the drive-in theme.

During the 1990s, several countries around the world honored the Thunderbird with postage stamps. "In 1988," notes Texan Dot Lang, another avid collector of Thunderbirdiana, "7-Up gave away several pink '57s plus pedal cars with the 7-Up logo. I have the grocery-store promotional display for that contest plus a cassette recording of the promotional songs. And I just acquired a lapel button from a 1981 A&W Root Beer contest in Canada, which offered a '56 Thunderbird as its top prize."

❏ AN AMERICAN CLASSIC
Not long after the two-seater was gone, the nation began to recognize what it had lost. *Today Show* host Dave Garroway, an auto enthusiast in his own right, referred on the air to the two-seater as "an American classic." Collectors were already buying and selling Early Birds in the 1960s. Today, the 1955-57 Thunderbirds are indisputably among the most desired and collected automobiles ever built. Of the 53,166 Early Birds produced, roughly 35,000 (66%) have been preserved. Thunderbirds from 1955-57 are so popular that, in Antique

Betty Boop takes her pup for a ride, and Snoopy seems unaware of Woodstock perched on his 1956 Bird's continental spare tire. Both cars contain wind-up music boxes.

Matchbox toys paid homage to Patsy Cline in 1996 with a limited edition of a special 1957 T-Bird toy. And a model Thunderbird pedal car with Crayola graphics was produced by Gearbox in 1999. The car in the foreground is a 1956 Bird without a continental kit.

Automobile Club of America (AACA) judging, they compete against each other in their own separate class. The only other cars with special classes are the Model T, Model A and 1932-48 Fords; the 1965-73 Mustang; the Chevrolet Corvette; and the 1955-58 full-sized Chevrolet.

Early Birds were an instant hit with Hollywood as well. Marilyn Monroe owned one. Eddie Fisher bought one for Debbie Reynolds. Longtime auto buff Clark Gable had a Paxton supercharger fitted to his personal 1955 Bird. The entertainment industry rediscovered the Thunderbird in the 1970s, when all things Fifties again became the height of fashion.

And Thunderbirds have appeared in many, many movies. Certainly the most famous was the white '56 hardtop from which Suzanne Somers beckoned Richard Dreyfuss in *American Graffiti*. Less widely remembered is the black '57 driven by Burt Reynolds in *The Man Who Loved Women*. A classic Thunderbird appeared with Robin Williams in *The Birdcage*, and a 1956 Bird went from gray to green in the eccentric

Plastic bathroom tissue holder was also available in blue, pink and yellow.

Once Santa got into a Thunderbird, he had a hard time going back to his sleigh. This Christmas ornament by Enesco is made of plastic, replicates 1956 Thunderbird with admirable accuracy.

Hollywood fantasy *Pleasantville.*

Little Birds cruised across the small screen as well. Investigator Paul Drake of *Perry Mason* and Susan Sullivan of *Falcon Crest* both tooled around in 1957 Birds. Claude Akins, himself something of a icon, drove a '56 T-Bird in *Movin'*

On. In *Vega$,* private eye Dan Tanna, played by Robert Urich, not only drove a '57 with a continental kit but parked it in his living room. Tony Franciosa co-starred with a '57 in *Matt Helm.* In *Roadhouse 66,* televised in 1984, Willem DaFoe drove a '55 Thunderbird.

In pop music, The Beach Boys paid a lasting tribute to the Thunderbird with *Fun, Fun, Fun ('Til Her Daddy Takes the T-Bird Away).* Less remembered is a group called the Thunderbirds, who posed in a '57 for an album cover. Conway Twitty put a green '56 on one of his

Male jewelry emblazoned with the Thunderbird theme has proved popular almost from the day the two-seater came out. The cuff links and tie tack below were made by Swank in the mid 1950s. And the belt buckles here are only three of dozens of designs produced down through the years.

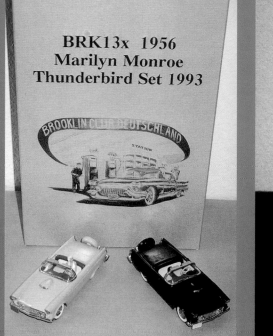

BRK13x 1956
Marilyn Monroe
Thunderbird Set 1993

Thunderbirds have always been linked to celebrities. In 1993, the German Brooklin toy club commissioned a commemorative of Marilyn Monroe, above, complete with pink and black T-Birds. A tiny figure of Marilyn was supplied by Omen Miniatures. At right, American Plastic Toys designed a T-Bird with Barbie in mind, but it's shown here with Mattel's Midge doll.

albums, and a recent compilation album titled *Wild Thing* pictures a girl, a beach and a '57 Thunderbird.

❑ THE TOYS ROLL ON
Miniature toys, models and other re-productions of the two-seater began to appear while the Early Bird was still in its infancy. "Tin-plate cars made in Japan underscored the immediate popularity of the Thunderbird," says collector Legel. Bandai and others had tin-lithograph

1955-56 T-Birds in production almost as soon as the cars came out. Some were friction-drive, others battery powered. One with batteries performed an elaborate sequence of opening and closing doors, flashing lights and forward motion. Another toy Bird came with a clear Lexan top.

According to some sources, Ford Division general manager Robert F. McNamara did consider a Thunderbird station wagon, but it took the Japanese to actually build

one. The wagon was a full five inches long and made of tin.

Post Cereal put one-piece toy Early Birds into breakfast boxes, complete with pre-production Fairlane trim! Another one-piece plastic toy, called the *Thunderstreak*, was for the most part accurately scaled and detailed but had airhorns on the hood and Buick-style portholes in the front fenders.

Modelmaker AMT, now a part of Ertl, produced the original

Spectacular gold-plated 1955 Thunderbird was conceived by Yat Ming to celebrate the arrival of the year 2000. Copies were handed out at swanky New Years parties throughout the world.

Ford dealer promo models of two-passenger Thunderbirds. A special-edition red '57 with white and copper interior was available free to anyone who visited a local Ford dealership and filled out the appropriate coupon. Some time later, AMT offered a '55 model kit for assembly. But given the widespread production of 1955-56 Thunderbird toys, notes Dr. Legel, model kits are surprisingly scarce. The few kits sold at the time of actual 1955-57 two-seater production seem to have been of poor quality.

One 1955 kit from Ideal was "powered" by a scale plastic Straight Eight, an engine configuration never used by Ford. A more accurate plastic 1956 Bird from Monogram and metal kits from both Monogram and Testors appeared in the 1970s, long after the real car had gone out of production.

By 1957, however, kit manufacturers were beginning to take notice of the Thunderbird's success. Renwall and Rigo launched 1:43-

Thunderbird bodies were and remain popular with slot-car racers. Gathered here, left to right, are a yellow Motorific 1956 Bird by Ideal circa 1960, a red 1:24-scale 1957 by AMT from its Turnpike Cruiser set, a white '57 Aurora in 1:43 scale and a Tyco HO-scale model from the 1980s in blue and white.

These plastic and rubber toy Thunderbirds were available in dimestores and cost only a few pennies each. Today, collectors often pay hundreds of times their original prices.

Ceramic mugs with pictures of Thunderbirds became available soon after the car itself went on sale. Like belt buckles, mugs come in a variety of shapes, sizes and patterns. A collector could concentrate on mugs alone and never run out of new discoveries.

scale models, and Revell introduced a 1:32 kit not long afterward. AMT produced a two-seater Thunderbird kit—and still does. Much later, of course, AMT offered a *Vega$* edition '57 with continental spare and an incongruously named "Here Comes the Judge" drag-race car powered by a blown 460 V8.

And by the early '60s, Thunderbirds appeared as slot cars, too. AMT modified its dealer model as a 1:24 motorized "Turnpike" car. Hawk Plastics offered a lightweight, flexible 1957 Bird body in 1:24 scale and, like many other slot-car bodies of the era, it was molded in clear plastic so the hobbyist could custom-paint it on the inside.

Tyco presented electric Thunderbirds in HO scale, and Aurora sold a slightly larger slot car. Ideal offered Motorific battery-powered slotsters for younger children. Bodies were interchangeable, each scaled to fit a roughly 1:43-scale chassis. The Motorific lineup included 1956 T-Bird bodies in at least five colors.

Busch Praline still makes surprisingly detailed Thunderbirds in a variety of colors, sized for HO train

layouts. MTH used to offer a model railcar that carried a couple of '57 Thunderbirds by Ertl. Collector Dot Lang mentions that T-Bird models and toys began to fade in popularity in the mid 1960s but then came roaring back in the '80s, "...and it's been going pretty steady ever since."

Several Pacific Rim producers have offered pull-back action T-Birds since the 1980s. A company called Fleetwood produced the *Vega$* Dan Tanna car with a pull cord. In the early

1990s, McDonald's gave away a windup Early Bird with a Happy Meal; in 1983 and again in 1991 the fast-food chain handed out Hot Wheels Thunderbirds and printed placemats with pictures of the toy. Taco Bell, Carl's Jr. and the Radio Grille have also used toy Thunderbirds in their promotions.

Major oil companies, including Texaco, Gulf and Shell, have likewise commissioned Thunderbird toys and models. Even the Pittsburgh

Lithographed tin toys from Japan captured essential features of the 1955 and '56 Thunderbirds, but collectors have yet to find a 1957. The red car's Lexan top is unusual and highly prized.

Produced as a birthday-party favor, the Cruisin' ensemble, opposite, includes a Thunderbird coloring book and crayons shaped like T-Birds. At top right, a pewter 1956 paperweight, 4.5 inches long, by Collectors Case. And below it is a polystone T-Bird clock made in China.

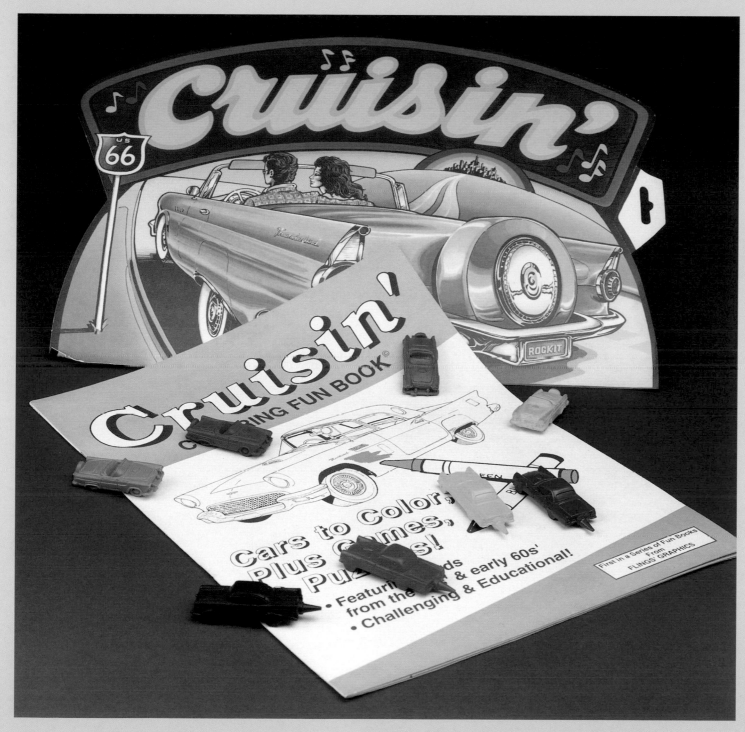

Steelers once put their stamp on a 1955 T-Bird model. Dr. Legel points out that Japanese tin-plate T-Birds were produced as recently as the 1980s and, just in the last decade, American Plastic Toys, Inc. manufactured a Barbie-sized 1957 Bird in pink, red or yellow, suitable for any 11.5-inch fashion doll.

Banthrico's slush-cast coin bank became a popular gift from financial institutions to their patrons. Customers often got such banks for opening new accounts.

❏ PEDAL CARS AND GOLF CARTS

Several manufacturers have made Thunderbird pedal cars. Then there are the electric Thunderbird Juniors, 1:4-scale replicas of cars from the 1950s and '60s. Ralph's Custom Golf Carts in California manufactured the Mini 'Bird, a golfcart that resembled a 1957 Thunderbird. The lower body of the Mini 'Bird came out surprisingly well, and the cart had a removable hardtop, complete with porthole. Golfbags rode on the rear bumper, much like the 1956 spare tire. Mini 'Bird production ended in 1997.

Among diecast Thunderbirds, Corgi produced the *Vega$ '57*, replete with continental kit, in both 1:43 and 1:64 scale. Matchbox also offered a *Vega$ '57*. Now that the TV show is fading from memory, Corgi has re-issued the model, but

Below are McDonald's premiums handed out with Kids Meals. At left, Texaco commissioned Gearbox to make nine-inch promotional models in three different colors: green, red and black.

with a figure of Elvis Presley and his guitar. Corgi is likewise expected to release a Marilyn Monroe Thunderbird set. Similarly, a German diecast collector club commissioned Brooklin to make model '56 Thunderbirds with a figure of Marilyn Monroe.

Dr. Legel has documented four different Matchbox/Hot Wheels castings: with and without porthole, without top and the slightly custom-ized "Classic Thunderbird." Limited production runs have been done as promotions for F.A.O. Schwarz, Service Merchandise (all chrome), J. C. Penney, Target and Coca-Cola. Pepsi-Cola has placed the company logo on miniature Birds.

Majorette, Ertl, Yat Ming, Racing Champions and Revell have all made larger-scale diecast Birds. So have Lonestar (England), Solido (France) and Tekno (Denmark). Rio produced a number of 1956 models, including a 1956 Daytona racer. Brooklin has produced a variety of diecast Thunderbirds, including commemoratives for the Classic Thunderbird Club International.

The Franklin and Danbury mints have offered 1:24-scale Thunderbirds; and Franklin did a 1:43 1956 model as well. This was part of its *Classic Cars of the Fifties* display-case set. In the late 1980s, Ertl produced a '57 in the original white-over-turquoise color scheme.

COOKIE JARS & MUSIC BOXES

But beyond even models and toys, the early Thunderbird has introduced itself into the very articles of every-

day living. Cookie jars make a good example. "There have been four styles that I can think of," asserts Dot Long, "all made in the 1980s and '90s and all depicting the '56 T-Bird." Other ceramics in the Thunderbird aviary have included banks, flower vases, music boxes, figurines, candy dishes, ashtrays, a soap dish holder, a pen holder, jewelry boxes, picture frames, coffee mugs and collector plates. Jim Beam offered Thunderbird decanters in five different colors; Ezra Brooks also offered a decanter set.

Mickey Mouse, Betty Boop and Snoopy can all be found driving ceramic '56s, with Minnie Mouse, Betty Boop's dog and Peanuts' bird Woodstock as their respective passengers. Banthrico has been making a 1955 Thunderbird metal coin bank since 1975, one that's often used to promote real banks and stores. Hertz, the car-rental company, sponsored a mantle clock in corporate yellow and blue depicting a T-Bird with Hertz license plates.

Texas-based printer Checks in the Mail offers a series of personalized checks called *Dream*

Hubley cast-metal Thunderbirds aren't rare, but to find one with its original box plus the plastic interior, top and trim pieces is unusual. These parts are mostly long lost in the sandbox. This same model also came in yellow, with a white interior.

In 1957, AMT supplied Ford dealers with highly detailed plastic promotional Thunderbird models. Some components, such as the windshield frame and steering wheel, were very delicate and rarely survived.

The cookie jar, above, was offered in 1990 by a California company called Scobey/Paleno.

Machines, all with wide-angle close-ups of popular 1950s quarter panels. The original collection consisted of a '59 Cadillac Eldorado, '57 Chevrolet Bel Air and '57 Thunderbird. The series is still available but, inexplicably, the Thunderbird was replaced a few years ago by a 1958 Buick Century. Go figure.

Meanwhile, the Berkeley, California-based Peaceable Kingdom Press even published a greeting card in which four cats drive a caricatured but recognizable '57 Thunderbird. Dot Lang has also documented a Thunderbird-shaped telephone, a T-Bird toilet-tissue holder, a Thunderbird "jukebox" that plays

Made of heavy, folded paper, this T-Bird is intended as an appealing container for school lunches.

CDs or 45-rpm records, a pinball machine with Thunderbird graphics, a range of different Thunderbird drinking glasses ("one was a Ford giveaway when the 1957s were new"), a glass Thunderbird pitcher by Couroc, an insulated gallon jug with Thunderbird script plus T-Bird serving trays.

Over the years, there have been Thunderbird wallpaper, needle-point patterns, hooked-rug kits, pot holders, refrigerator magnets, post-cards, matchbook covers, wind-chimes and several Zippo cigarette lighters. "There's a tin box on the market now, with the Coca-Cola logo and a picture of a gas station with a 1956 T-Bird behind the pumps," says Dot Lang. "And I recently picked up some Thunderbird swizzle sticks."

To this list Steve Legel adds a Thunderbird lint brush, coin bank, watch, knife, belt buckles, soft-drink cups and salt shakers. He's even seen Thunderbirds on gambling chips, probably at the Thunderbird Hotel in Las Vegas and the Thunderbird Resort near Reno. Then there are Thunderbird Christmas ornaments

from Hallmark, Enesco, Carlton, Kurt Adler and Schmid, the latter featuring those other quintessential American icons, Mickey and Minnie Mouse. Lemax issued a snow-village-scale '55 in 1998; Dept. 56 followed up with their own '55 for 1999. And the industry isn't slowing down. Legel points out that 1999 saw a particularly large number of new T-Bird issues, including a new AM/FM radio and a motorized toy from the motion picture *Toy Story II*.

Lang adds the just-issued, boxed set of auto polish and cleaner

from Duragloss. On the lid of the box and on the bottles inside is the depiction of a black 1956 Bird with a white top.

And what's coming down the road? Well, Maisto has already issued 1:18 and 1:24 scale models of the 1999 Thunderbird concept car. They're painted pale yellow. Then for the 2000 show season, black and coral versions were issued. Maisto also sells the 1:43 models under the *Road & Track* label. And AMT/Ertl offers a 1:25 snap-together kit of the 2002 Bird as well. ❏

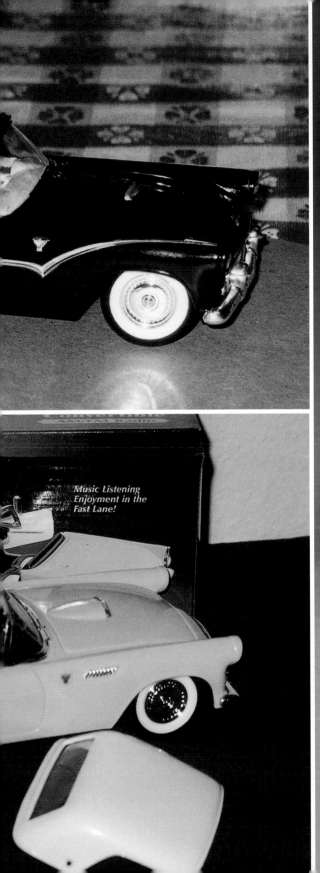

SENSATIONS™

50ˢ Taillight Message Clip

Music Listening Enjoyment in the Fast Lane!

T BIRD I

From far left: Danish Tekno model with box, rare pre-intro Fairlane Bird, yellow AM/FM radio with controls in trunk and, above, refrigerator message holder. Pushbutton in center of spare makes tail lamps blink.

Clearly, collectors of Thunderbird memorabilia and iconography tend to favor items having to do with the 1955-57 model years—so much so that relatively few collectibles celebrate the Squarebird and later cars. Yet Thunderbird mobilia from 1958 to the present are slowly being recognized.

Not surprisingly, most 1958 Thunderbird ads emphasized the car's new-found seating capacity. As early as 1962, *Car and Driver* commented that the Thunderbird's "excellent sales record and grasp on the public's imagination are unequaled among U.S. production cars." The Vintage Thunderbird Club International (VCTI), founded in 1968, began to collect and preserve Squarebirds when those cars were still less than 10 years old.

From 1959 to 1963, Thunderbird advertising had a softer, richer, more sophisticated style. To underscore performance, one ad was headlined, "Hill? What hill?" A later ad highlighted the 1969 model's electric sunroof and four doors.

Four-place Thunderbirds occasionally show up as toys or models but much less often than the two-place originals. "There's not a whole lot after '63 until you get to the NASCAR T-Birds," mentions Dr. Legel. And we haven't even begun to count the number of toys, models and collectibles depicting the NASCAR Thunderbirds of the 1980s and '90s.

But later Birds have also been featured on

T-Birds painted on an ostrich egg.

TV and in movies. The painfully hip private eyes from *77 Sunset Strip* parked their Squarebird at Dino's, a rat-pack bar and eatery in Hollywood.

Then in 1998, Dennis Farina as detective Buddy Farro drove a '63 convertible. Thelma and Louise took their final leap in a '66 convertible. Mister Mister drove a '59 while lamenting their *Broken Wings* in an early-'80s music video. Bill Nye the *Science Guy* drove a red '64 convertible in several episodes. In a show about invertebrate animals, Nye cited the Thunderbird's unibody as an example of a manmade exoskeleton.

Department stores seemed to appreciate the 1967-71 big-Ford-based Birds. In 1967,

Abercrombie & Fitch commissioned half a dozen mobile business offices based on the two-door Thunderbird Landau, with a telephone (an exotic automobile accessory back then), writing tables and reading lamps for the rear compartment, plus extensive wood trim and a power footrest for the front-seat passenger. Gold highlights, color-keyed steel wheels and special lighting bejeweled the exterior. The conversions were actually performed by Dearborn Steel Tubing. Neiman Marcus offered His-and-Hers Thunderbirds in their 1970 Christmas book. Outfitted with telephones and tape recorders, each pair cost $25,000.

Collector interest came late to the 1967-71 Thunderbird, but it has come at last. The VTCI officially recognized this generation as collectible in 1995. By then, however, few remained. One estimate pegs the number of surviving 1967's at less than 1000. The survival rate of four-door models has been particularly low.

Thunderbirds from 1972 on have yet to inspire collectors, but it's only a matter of time. The basket-handle Birds of 1977-79, particularly, show all the earmarks of collector magnetism: good performance, popularity when new and a look that's stood the test of time. After that, 1983-88 Turbo Coupes and 1989-96 Super Coupes are also likely to inspire a following. Both generations were styling pioneers, and both offer outstanding performance. ❏

Two classics: a 1955 Thunderbird diecast metal model in 1:18 scale alongside the 1999 Maisto concept car.

6

THE BIRD FLIES

Ford deliberately did not promote the 1955-57 two-seater as a sports/racing car, yet the company did campaign Early Birds in speed-record attempts—and with gratifying success. At NASCAR's Daytona Speed Weeks in February 1955, *Mechanix Illustrated* auto editor Tom

At Daytona Speed Weeks in 1956, Chuck Daigh in a Ford-sponsored Thunderbird clocked a record 92.142 mph for the standing mile but was disqualified due to a technical mixup. Daigh returned two days later and averaged 88.779 mph, fastest standing mile of that year's trials.

McCahill entered an essentially stock Thunderbird, which driver Joe Ferguson pushed to 124.633 mph, a speed bettered only by a Jaguar XK-120M.

In '56, a Thunderbird prepared by racing legend Peter De Paolo and piloted by Chuck Daigh took that season's standing-mile trophy at 88.779 mph. DePaolo carefully blueprinted the Thunderbird's twin-carburetor V8, which probably developed some 30 horsepower more than its advertised 230 bhp. Bodyman Dwight (Whitey) Clayton shaved everything off the Bird that didn't look aerodynamic.

He also fabricated an aluminum tonneau cover, a tiny competition windscreen, and he even put mixing bowls over the headlights to improve air penetration. That year, too, a privately entered Thunderbird placed second in the flying mile at 87.889 mph, comfortably ahead of John Fitch's factory-backed Corvette. Fitch did take top-speed honors a few days later at 145.5 mph.

Daigh and DePaolo returned to Daytona in '57 with two highly modified Thunderbirds, nicknamed

In the mid 1950s, just about anyone who was able to afford the modest entry fee could run his car at Daytona during Speed Weeks. Here, an unidentified, privately owned 1956 Thunderbird–most likely driven down from Michigan–was stripped of non-essentials like bumpers, windshield, hubcaps, etc. The owner then snapped on a tonneau cover and took off down the beach.

Another private entry, again a 1956 model, takes the flag at the beginning of Daytona's flying mile. That year, Andy Hotten's Thunderbird hit 134.404 mph and Merritt Brown's went 122.491. Then in 1957, a modified Battlebird driven by Danny Eames averaged 160.356 mph.

"Battlebirds." These were set up to do battle primarily against the Corvettes. Each Battlebird was equipped with aluminum body panels, full bellypans, four-speed transmissions (probably Jaguar) and Halibrand quick-change rear axles. Battlebirds had auxiliary fast-fill fuel tanks, suggesting that they might later enter the 12-hour sports car race at Sebring.

One Battlebird was powered by a fuel-injected Lincoln 430-cid V8. The second used a Thunderbird 312 V8, again with Hilborn fuel injection plus a McCulloch supercharger. Danny Eames drove the Lincoln-powered car to an average of 98.065 mph through the standing mile, then nearly equaled that with the 312-cid Bird at 97.933 mph. Buck Baker's 366-cid Corvette SR2 couldn't touch either mark.

In the flying mile, Eames clocked the fastest time of the 1957 meet, 160.356 mph in the Lincoln-engined Bird. Baker trailed at 152.866 mph. The 283-cid Corvettes competed in a different class, but a stock Thunderbird privately entered by Harold Mauk dis-patched them, too, at 138.775 mph.

Daytona Speed Weeks in 1957 also included a road race at the New Smyrna Beach airport. Curtis Turner, in the Lincoln-engined Battlebird, was black-flagged for allegedly trying to ram Carroll Shelby's 4.9-liter Ferrari. Shelby eventually won the race, but Marvin Panch in the 312 Battlebird finished second. Second behind a Ferrari was almost like winning, especially since the T-Bird came in well ahead of any Corvette. But the Battlebirds didn't attempt Sebring.

As well as the T-Birds performed, Speed Weeks confirmed that Ford's little two-seaters weren't really suited to oval-track racing. And while a handful of Early Birds did compete in stock-car events, their performance was limited by poor aerodynamics and brake fade.

❏ SQUAREBIRDS GO RACING

The unibodied Squarebird fared better, although in 1958, race-car builders favored Ford's Custom 300 coupes. But for 1959, and for a number of reasons, many of them switched to that year's Thunderbird.

First, the T-Bird's rear leaf springs gave better cornering control than the previous coils. Second, the 430 V8 made for terrific acceleration. Third, Ford stretched the 300's wheelbase to 118 inches, and while the Squarebird weighed more than a Ford coupe, its lower stance and shorter wheelbase gave it an edge, especially after stripping out the Thunderbird's luxury equipment.

Race-car builders Holman & Moody fortified the 1959 Thunderbird with heavy-duty springs, shocks, spindles and brakes. They also fitted their cars with full roll cages and oversized fuel tanks. Visually, though, these racing Squarebirds deviated remarkably little from their showroom brethren.

In 1959, NASCAR ran the first 500-mile race at the then-new

Upper left, one of the 1957 Battlebirds, with Fireball Roberts driving, duels with a Jaguar XK-SS on an unidentified track in 1959. Above, Ford commissioned Holman & Moody to prepare eight 1959 Thunderbirds for NASCAR. This one, driven by Cotton Owens, carries the nickname "Thunder-Chick."

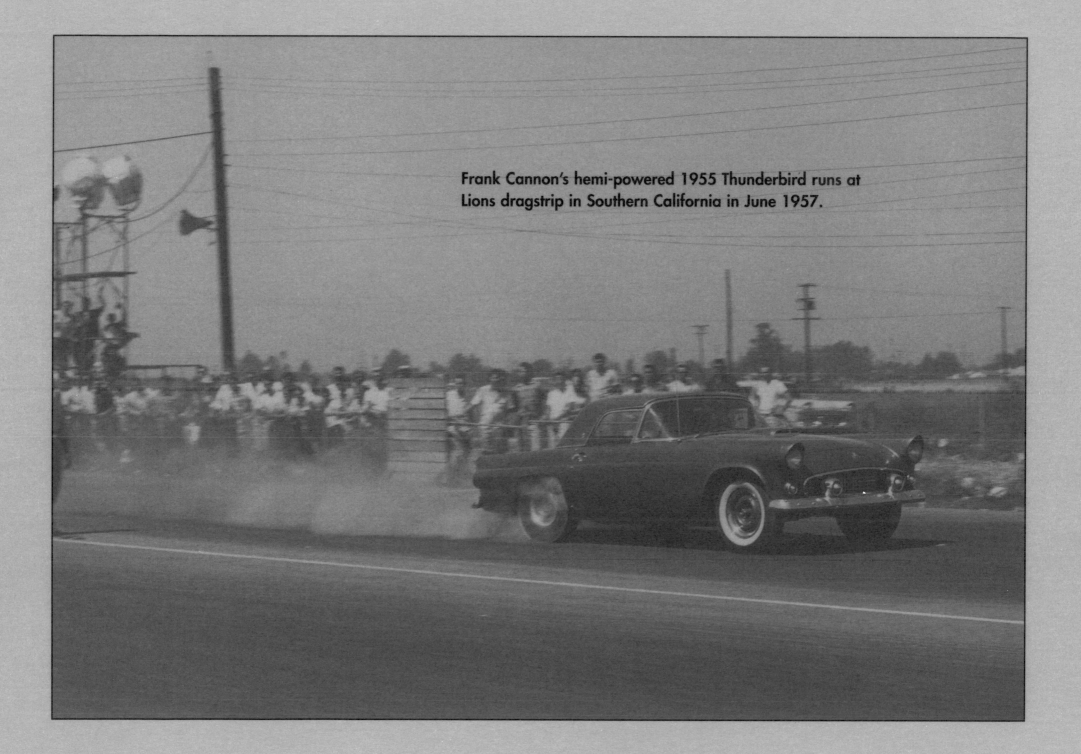

Frank Cannon's hemi-powered 1955 Thunderbird runs at
Lions dragstrip in Southern California in June 1957.

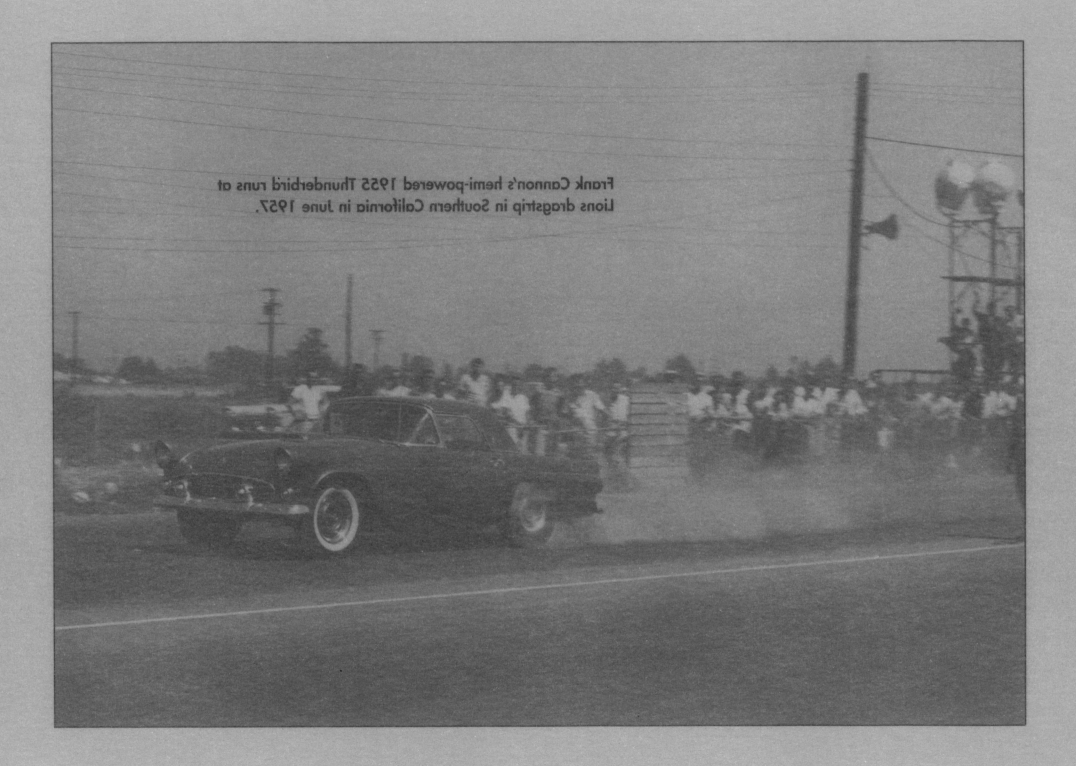

Here Johnny Beauchamp "wins" the first Daytona 500 in T-Bird #73. Three days later he lost the decision to Lee Petty's Olds #42. At right, two generations of Wayne Torkelson's Thunderbird drag machine–recent at top, early below.

Daytona International Speedway. In that event, driver Johnny Beauchamp in a Holman & Moody T-Bird battled it out to a photo finish with Lee Petty in an Oldsmobile. That fateful final picture showed Beauchamp, Petty and a Chevrolet driven by Joe Weatherly (one lap behind) crossing the finish line three abreast. Bill France and NASCAR officials studied that photo for three days before awarding the trophy to Petty. They

Frank Cannon and Art Chrisman, above, inspect the fuel-injected 454 Chrysler hemi V8 Chrisman put in Cannon's 1955 Thunderbird. The unbeatable Cannon turned 116 mph in the quarter mile. Another potent T-Bird, right, belonged to speed shop owner Bill Coon, who ran a sohc Ford 427. Coon topped 130 mph and won numerous honors in NHRA competition events.

gave Beauchamp second place, with other T-Birds finishing eighth, ninth and 13th.

By the end of the 1959 season, Thunderbirds had scored six Grand National victories, versus eight for Ford coupes and 14 for Chevrolets (several Chevys were the lighter 1957 models). In the convertible division, Thunderbirds tied their sedan stablemates with five wins each, while ragtop Chevrolets took nine firsts. So the Blue Oval and the Bow Tie ended up with an equal number of victories that year.

Six 1959 Holman & Moody Thunderbirds continued to run in Grand National throughout the 1960 season, along with a scattering of 1960 Birds from a range of less well-known constructors. But the Squarebird's glory days were over, because factory-backed Pontiacs now dominated all of stock-car racing. A few Thunderbirds still competed on short tracks into the Sixties, but the marque pretty much bowed out of top-flight NASCAR events, at

Knot Farrington's street-legal 1956 Bird, above, topped 173 mph at Bonneville in 1959. Same car and driver returned in 1963, this time with the streamlined body, below, and clocked 241 mph. Farrington still owns this car.

least for the foreseeable future.

Thunderbirds began to drift back in 1977. The '77 Thunderbird was a full 900 pounds lighter than the 1976 model, and that attracted drivers Bobby Allison, Dick Brooks and Jody Ridley to campaign Birds in 1978 Grand National competition. Allison's Bud Moore-prepared Thunderbird #15 won, among other events, the NAPA 400 at Riverside, California. In that race, Allison's clutch linkage broke, but he beat the second-place car by nearly 33 seconds anyway. Allison continued to campaign his T-Bird throughout 1979, placing second at the Southern 500 in Bristol, Tennessee.

❑ RISE OF THE AEROBIRD

The early to mid 1980s saw the rise of the Aerobird, which quickly proved the superiority of its slippery shape. In 1982-97, Thunderbirds won more than 150 races in NASCAR's top division, including four Daytona 500s. In 1985 alone, Georgian Bill Elliott drove his Coors-Melling Thunderbird to 11 super-speedway victories, including the Daytona 500, the Winston 500 at

Bobby Allison's 1979 Thunderbird, above, trails Johnny Parsons' Monte Carlo at North Wilkesboro in September 1980. Below, Kyle Petty's 1985 Aerobird was one of several prepared by Woods Racing.

Ricky Rudd in his 1985 Thunderbird, above and below, won five Winston Cup races in that and the following two seasons. Rudd's cars were prepared by Bud Moore Engineering and crew chief/mechanic Wadell Wilson.

Cale Yarbrough and million-dollar Bill Elliott, above, cruise down the Daytona straight. At right, two scenes from Sears Point, June 1989: Davey Allison's #28 at speed and fast work in the Thunderbird pits.

Alan Kulwicki's #7 Thunderbird leads Davey Allison's #28 at Sears Point, 1989. Three years later, Kulwicki took the Winston Cup championship. Both he and Allison died in 1993 in separate private air crashes.

Left, Rusty Wallace in Thunderbird #2 won 10 Winston Cup races in 1994. Here, Jeff Burton stays the course at the Daytona 500, 1995.

Talladega and the Southern 500 at Darlington. That earned him a $1 million bonus, offered by series sponsor R.J. Reynolds to any driver who could win three of NASCAR's four longest races (the fourth being the World 600 at Charlotte, where Elliott stumbled to 18th with tire and brake problems).

R.J. Reynolds hadn't expected to ever award the special prize, much less pay it out in the first season. And as it turned out, the tobacco company didn't have to pay it again for another 12 years, until Chevrolet's Jeff Gordon won the

prize in 1987. After that, R.J. Reynolds withdrew the bonus. Elliott and his Aerobird, however, went on to win the series championship in 1988.

❏ OTHER FORMS OF SPEED

Meanwhile and throughout the years, Thunderbirds had also made a name for themselves in drag racing and at Bonneville. Back in the 1950s, legendary hot rodder Art Chrisman specialized in engine swaps and performance tuneups. One of the cars he breathed on was Frank Cannon's 1955 Thunderbird.

After Cannon had been consistently beaten in local NHRA (National Hot Rod Association) events, Cannon drove the McCulloch-supercharged Bird into Chrisman's shop in Compton, California and asked for help. Chrisman built him a new airbox that blew through the carburetors, and on the next weekend, Cannon ran 109 mph in the quarter mile, versus 104 or so for the competition. Even at that, Cannon wanted more, so Chrisman suggested installing a Chrysler hemi V8.

"We bought a brand-new hemi," recalled Chrisman many

years later, "and I bored and stroked it to 454 cubic inches, added an Isky cam, Hilborn injectors and a Vertex magneto." Then on six-inch slicks, using second and high gears only, Cannon posted a best time of 116 mph and never lost a race after that.

During the 1960s, William (Bill) Coon, a speed shop owner from Plymouth, Michigan campaigned a 1957 Thunderbird powered by one of the most potent of all Detroit passenger-car V8s: Ford's single-overhead-cam 427. This engine delivered no fewer than 650

Brett Bodine, above, runs the Daytona 500 in 1995. At right, Bill Elliott in his #9 Thunderbird.

horsepower. Coon reworked the Bird's suspension to give it wheel-standing weight transfer, resulting in time slips in the 10.60-second range at 130 mph. Coon's cammer competed in the B/Modified Sports class and won numerous honors, including wins at the 1967 NHRA Winternationals and Springnationals drag fests.

Then, in the late 1980s, the IHRA created the Pro Modified drag-racing class to accommodate fiberglass replicas of 1950s and '60s passenger cars. One such vehicle was (and still is) the Torkelson family's "fanglastic" 1955 Thunderbird. Wayne Torkelson Jr. and Sr., a father/son team that races out of California and Ohio respectively, put together a 2700-pound racer on a special tubular frame. For power, they installed a GMC 4-71-blown, 526-cid, Alan Root-built 429 Ford V8. The engine runs on alcohol and transmits power through a Lenco four-speed planetary transmission, the result being that the Torkelsons' plastic-bodied Thunderbird posted an all-time personal best of 6.30 seconds at 220 mph in the quarter

mile at Maryland International Raceway in 1999. The Torkelsons still campaign this car regularly.

Thunderbirds likewise made a name for themselves at the Bonneville salt flats in Utah. L.W.

(Knot) Farrington, a garage owner from New Orleans, brought his 1956 T-Bird to Bonneville in 1959 and tripped the clocks at 173 mph, some 16 mph faster than the then-existing A/Sports class record.

Farrington's metal-bodied Thunderbird was powered by a 1956 Chrysler hemi V8.

Four years later, in 1963, Farrington made his final run on the salt with the same car. He'd radical-

King Racing's pit crew quickly refreshes Brett Bodine's Thunderbird at 1994 Brickyard 400.

ly altered it to make the body more aerodynamic. This included fabricating a new tail section out of two 1957 Dodge station-wagon roofs, rounding off the nose and installing a full bellypan.

Knot Farrington set the 454-cid hemi V8 back in the frame as far as rules allowed and fitted it with a 6-71 GMC supercharger. Then, totally street legal—with operating headlights, horn, starter and generator—the Thunderbird took to the salt and was timed at over 241 mph, making it the fastest of its genre of all time. Farrington, like Torkelson, still owns this legendary Thunderbird.

❑ THE FINAL YEARS
Back on the ovals, the 1989-97 Thunderbirds proved themselves every bit as raceable as the preceding Aerobirds. The year 1992 was particularly memorable for Ford fans, with Thunderbirds finishing first through fourth at Daytona, driver Alan Kulwicki capturing the Winston Cup title and Birds winning 16 of 29 Winston Cup events. This earned Ford Motor Co. its 10th manufacturer's championship; the

company's first since the '69 season.

Twenty Thunderbird wins in '94 brought the manufacturer's title home to Ford for the 11th time. Elliott continued to be a driving force for Ford, joined by Geoff Bodine, Mark Martin, Rusty Wallace and Ernie Irvan.

On 16 June 1997, in the Thunderbird coupe's final year, cars driven by Irvan, Elliott, Martin and Ted Musgrove swept the top four places in the Miller 400 at Michigan International Raceway, after which the Thunderbird retired from NASCAR with Ford's 12th manufac-

turer's championship. In February 1998, the Ford Taurus took up where the Thunderbirds left off.

Success in NASCAR and on the drag strip has sparked interest in groups like the Super Coupe Club of America, which offers technical assistance on outfitting 1989-97

Thunderbirds for amateur racing. And a variety of companies now carry accessories ranging from superchargers to suspension upgrades. So for a car that Ford never intended to race, the Thunderbird has posted some rousing speeds and surprising victories. ❑

Geoff Bodine's winning ways were crucial to Ford's 12th manufacturer's championship by the time of the Thunderbird's discontinuance in 1997.

2002 THUNDERBIRD
STANDARD EQUIPMENT

Powertrain
3.9-liter aluminum V8 with dual overhead cams and four valves per cylinder
Five-speed automatic transmission
Next-generation powertrain electronic controller module
Fail-safe cooling system with hydraulically driven fan

Chassis
Variable-ratio, variable-assist power steering
Four-wheel vented disc brakes with ABS and electronic proportioning
Dual-piston, cast-aluminum front brake calipers
Lightweight alloy suspension components
Front and rear SLA suspension with anti-dive/anti-lift tuning
Tubular steel front and rear stabilizer bars
Collapsible two-piece driveshaft
Isolated rear subframe with three-point elastomeric mounts
Nodular iron rear axle carrier
Eighteen-gallon fuel tank

Wheels and tires
17 x 7.5-inch painted cast-aluminum wheels
P235/50VR17 all-season blackwall tires
17-inch mini spare tire and aluminum wheel

Exterior features
Power convertible cloth top with heated glass rear window

Dual power mirrors
Clear lens headlamps with integral parking lamps and turn indicators
Bright windshield molding and rear license plate surround
Color-keyed rocker moldings

Interior features
Leather seating surfaces
Leather-wrapped steering wheel and automatic shift handle
Power six-way driver's seat
Power two-way passenger seat
Tilt/recline seatbacks
Manual lumbar adjustment for driver's seat
Driver/passenger center armrest with console storage
Dual cup holders
Locking glovebox with convenience hook
Carpeted floor area
Driver's foot rest
Door trim panel with soft feel insert
Fully trimmed luggage compartment

Safety and security
Driver airbag
Passenger airbag with deactivation switch
Two-way adjustable head restraints
Driver and passenger three-point safety harnesses
Driver and passenger side airbags
ISOFIX child restraint/top tether on passenger seat
Automatic locking retractor on passenger restraint
Gearshift interlock
Power door locks
Remote keyless entry
Master key/single key system

SecuriLock theft deterrent system
Perimeter anti-theft system

Comfort and convenience
Power windows
One-touch-down driver's window
Cruise control
Power tilt/telescope steering column
Illuminated entry with theater dimming
Courtesy lamps in footwell, rearview mirror
Lighted trunk and glovebox
Dual map lights
Dome light integrated with rearview mirror
Automatic headlamp on/off with adjustable time delay
Speed-sensitive, variable, intermittent windshield wipers
Smart Locks to prevent locking keys in car
Auto locks
Day/night rearview mirror
Dual multi-adjustable sunvisors with illuminated vanity mirrors
Solar-tint windshield, side glass and rear window
Gradient tint band on windshield
Rear window defroster
Gas cylinder decklid supports
Delayed accessory power shutoff
Battery saver

Audio
Audiophile sound system
AM/FM stereo CDX6 with six-disc, in-dash CD changer
Steering-wheel-mounted redundant audio controls
Windshield mounted antenna

Climate control
Dual automatic temperature control
Side window demisters
Dual-vane registers with positive shutoffs

Instrument panel
Soft instrument panel with lower portion in accent interior color
Large display, cluster graphics with auxiliary single character E-PRNDL
Speedometer calibrated in miles and kilometers per hour
Odometer with dual trip display
Rotary headlamp switch
Illuminated lighter and switches
Integrated, continuous-display digital clock in radio

Canadian cars also receive:
Metric speedometer
Daytime running lights
Engine block heater

2002 THUNDERBIRD OPTIONAL EQUIPMENT

Removable top with heated glass rear window
Parking lamps
Interior color accent package
Engine block heater
17 x 7.5-inch chromed cast-aluminum wheels
Traction control

ACKNOWLEDGEMENT AND APPRECIATION

ASG Renaissance, Gil Baumgartner, Dan Bedore, Anka Brazzell, Ray Brock, Bill Buffa, Campbell & Co., Rich Carlson, Mark D. Conforzi, Ray Day, Mickey D'Armi, Daytona Racing Archives, Regis D. Enright, Dan Erickson, Afaf Farrah, Fred T. Finney, Ford Photomedia, Doug Gaffka, Bill George, Dave Geraci, Nancy L. Gioia, Gloria Gomah, Goodyear Tire & Rubber Co., Henry Ford Museum and Greenfield Village, Samantha Hunt, International Speedway Corp., John Jelinek, John Katz, Lee Kelley, Kevin Kennedy, Rich Kisler, Larry Kooiman, Kenneth K. Kohrs, Dot Lang, John Larabell, Bob Leach, Dr. Steve Legel, Doyle D. Letson, Paula Lewis, Jeff Loudermilk, LucasFilms, Buz McKim, Leslie A. Miller, Dan Murray, Neiman Marcus Inc., Chuck Nerpel, Mike O'Sullivan, Brian F. Rathsburg, Ginger Reeder, Eric Rickman, Dorothy Rogan, Whitney Said, Suzanne Somers, Frank & Cathy Stubbs, Carole A. Swartz, Keith Tolman, Wayne Torkelson, Universal Studios, Jim Walesch, Don Warneke, T. Taylor Warren, Dean Weber, Robert F. Widmer, Ken Zino.

Book art direction by Michelle Manos. Text for Chapters Four, Five and Six by John F. Katz.

Thunderbird

The infamous 1953 "Burnetti," named for Ford chief engineer Bill Burnett, served as the running prototype for the first Thunderbird. Burnett and his team cut apart a 1953 Ford coupe and welded the frame and body panels back together to approximate the dimensions and handling characteristics of the 1955 Thunderbird.

The infamous 1953 "Burnetti," named for Ford chief engineer Bill Burnett, served as the running prototype for the first Thunderbird. Burnett and his team cut apart a 1953 Ford coupe and welded the frame and body panels back together to approximate the dimensions and handling characteristics of the 1955 Thunderbird.